T5-CQD-659

The Way to Spiritual Strength

In the Face of

Temptation

The Way to Spiritual Strength

In the Face of

Temptation

Bob Mumford

Creation House
Altamonte Springs, Florida

Creation House
Strang Communications Company
190 N. Westmonte Drive
Altamonte Springs, FL 32714
(305) 869-5005

Unless otherwise noted, all Scripture references are taken from the New American Standard Bible, copyright by The Lockman Foundation, 1960, 1962, 1963, 1968, 1971, 1972, 1973, 1975, 1977.

Verses marked Amplified are taken from the Amplified New Testament, copyright The Lockman Foundation 1954, 1958.

Verses marked TLB are taken from The Living Bible, copyright 1971 by Tyndale House Publishers, Wheaton, Illinois. Used by permission.

First Printing, July 1987
Second Printing, December 1987

To all Christians who have
unnecessarily languished in the wilderness because
they misunderstood God's ways.

Contents

Introduction

When the prophet Hosea cried, "My people are destroyed for lack of knowledge" (4:6), he penetrated the need of God's people of every generation. We must be instructed in His ways; we must come to understand that God works on given principles.

This book on temptation is designed to examine God's ways and learn His principles of operation. It is not a theological discourse on the Garden of Eden. Rather it is a manual of practical instruction. Learning these skills can help you understand biblical truths and bring you into the abundant supply God has for His children.

One marvelous thing that happens as you study the Scriptures is that you discover its organic nature. It is like a tree: the roots are the Old Testament; the trunk is the Lord Jesus Christ; the branches and fruit are the twenty-seven books of the New Testament. If you touch any one word or verse at the very top of the tree, you find it organically attached to the root system in the Old Testament.

The organic nature of the Scriptures is a blessing in that it gives us reason to trust the integrity of the Word. Because it is organic, the whole Bible can be correctly interpreted around any one of many themes. For instance, I can take the word *covenant* and, starting in Genesis, arrange the whole Bible into an understanding and application of that word. This has been done and it is called *covenantal theology*.

But a problem arises when you increase the number of words around which the whole Bible is interpreted. These might include *the Holy Spirit*, *redemption*, *Messiah*, *the church*, *the kingdom of God*. To my amazement, I found that the whole Bible can easily be interpreted and arranged around the theme of *temptation*. From Genesis 3 to Revelation 22 there is a powerful unfolding of a most important theme: how Satan tempts and God tests His people.

Because the Bible unfolds beautifully around a particular word, it is easy to assume that it is the central and most important theme in the whole Bible. But our challenge is to interpret Scriptures without an overemphasis on one particular theme.

As we approach an intensive look at trial and temptation, let us be careful not to take the part as being the whole. A sixteen-week instruction in algebra is not all there is to mathematics. An intensive study of temptation, however valuable, is not all there is to walking with the Lord in peace and progress.

There are three objectives to this book:

1. To feed, strengthen and encourage new believers by showing fundamental lessons that will enable them

to walk as straight as they are able into as large a place of maturity and usefulness as they desire. My own response upon completing this book was, "I wish I had known this thirty years ago!"

2. To fill in the gaps, assumptions and misunderstandings that abound in the church regarding the process and purpose of temptation. A casual reading of this book should show that an unclear or haphazard approach to trial and temptation is expensive, causing a cyclical rather than linear approach to our Christian experience.

3. To provide clear teaching for the more advanced believer, who already walks with the Lord in a consistent manner yet suspects that there are some needed answers in certain areas. I trust that I have provided at least some of those answers. Most of them have been hammered out on the anvil of God's dealings in my own life.

Like others, I can testify to a life that has been changed. God's provisions for me in physical, financial and spiritual realms have been according to His promise. These have not come without an element of struggle, and that is why I share these experiences.

Little claim is made for originality. I am deeply indebted to a small book entitled *Temptation* by Dietrich Bonhoeffer. For me it was the beginning of the end of a long and desperate search for meaning to the turbulence that my hunger for God seemed to precipitate. As one who reads much, listens intently and makes profuse notes, I want to acknowledge my dependence upon the men, women and ministries that have made contributions to my journey.

My prayer is that the lessons of this book will be so quickened by the Holy Spirit that readers will "count it all joy" when trial or temptation is their portion!

Genuine appreciation is due to Stephen Strang of Creation House books and to my editor, Bert Ghezzi of Creation House, whose encouragement and professional skills helped make this book a reality. Gratitude unbounded is extended to my wife, Judy, for giving her hours to me for this book and to my daughter Keren Kilgore who laboriously interpreted my handwriting onto the word processor.

O God, our Father, may You be pleased to use this writing in Your own mysterious way—ministering to those tossed on the stormy sea of temptation.

In Jesus' name, Amen.

Bob Mumford
P.O. Box 13459
San Rafael, CA 94913

chapter one

Temptation in Perspective

W hile you were in New York, I came mighty close to breaking the promise I gave you about not using the car while you were away," a young man said to his father. "You left the keys on the kitchen counter and I carried them around in my pocket for three days fighting the temptation."

The father smiled. "Son, there's nothing like temptation to show you what you'll do if you are given the opportunity!"

As our heavenly Father views it, temptation serves an essential purpose. It shows us what we are and where we stand; and it plays an important part in what we will be in the future. *Temptation is a factor in the psychological and spiritual growth process we must go through if we are to become mature individuals, capable of living full and meaningful lives.*

Temptation always triggers a choice and provokes a

definite stand or action. As in the case of the young man and the car keys, the keys on the kitchen counter presented the temptation that forced him to make a difficult and very important decision. Should he disobey his father and commit an act of irresponsibility which would make it psychologically easier to repeat this kind of choice? Or should he—by his obedience—establish the pattern for mature and wise decisions in the future?

How we face temptation affects every area of our personal experience. To understand more about the nature of temptation and its definite purpose is of vital importance.

Unfortunately, *temptation* is one of the most misunderstood words in our language. It is thought of as something to be avoided at all cost—something dangerous that will cause much pain or trouble or something that will surely lead us into wrongdoing.

Temptation may lead to these things, but only if we make the definite choice in that direction. Temptation is not the cause of trouble or wrongdoing. It just presents us with a choice. To blame my wrongdoing on temptation ("I wouldn't have done it if I hadn't been tempted!") is as ridiculous as saying, "I wouldn't have gotten a ticket if the light hadn't changed to red just before I got to the intersection."

Who was to blame for the ticket—you or the red light? The light only served to present you with a quick choice: Should I stop and obey the law or hurry through to save a minute—and make myself liable to face the consequences? The decision was entirely yours.

Understanding how temptation functions can help us face it differently—and can change our lives. When we Christians are honest with ourselves, we are forced to admit that there is a noticeable discrepancy between the Christian life as we experience it, and what we—down deep in our hearts—hope it can be. I say *hope*, because some of us aren't even sure that the Christian life *can* be much different.

The discrepancy between the beautiful promises in the Bible and the lives of many Christians is explained by some who say that the beautiful promises refer only to heaven. This is termed *pie-in-the-sky religion*, and it doesn't do much to help us solve our problems here and now. Paul refused this kind of escapism when he emphasized the now aspect of the Christian life in Romans 5:17:

> By the transgression of the one [Adam], death reigned through the one, much more those who receive the abundance of grace and of the gift of righteousness will reign in life through the One, Jesus Christ.

Real Christianity is when Bible promises become reality. This is how it was meant to be. An overabundance of God's promises (without realizing their provisions) brought me to a place where I refused to seek or accept another biblical promise until the ones I already knew became functional.

Knowing all the promises in the Bible by memory doesn't make the provisions automatically ours. I know Christians who go around quoting, "There is therefore now no condemnation for those who are in Christ Jesus" (Rom. 8:1). Yet they live under constant condemnation, as if they must carry the guilt of their old sins with them to the grave. I know others who quote scriptures about having joy in their hearts—and they are the saddest, most joyless creatures I have ever met! Still others know all the scriptures telling how we can love each other. However, they live in marriages that are on the verge of breakup, are unable to communicate love to their own children and have continual difficulties in business relationships.

Can God heal the brokenhearted? Effect recovery to the sick? Bring love to the lonely and bitter? Save the lost? Set free those who are in misery? Repair broken relationships? *Can* He bring love, joy and laughter into gray, empty lives? Make families one in love and spirit? *Can* He meet your particular need? Answer your particular prayer? Fulfill the particular promise you have cherished for years? *Can* He—or *can't* He? Is the Bible true or is it a bunch of fairy tales—just something to comfort us in this world of problems? Is religion a crutch for the weak who cannot face reality?

I believe firmly that the Bible is true—every word of it; and I have seen enough of those promises turned into real provision over the last years to know—without the least doubt—that behind the words of the Bible stands our all-powerful and loving Father, who not only can make His words good but wants to see this happen!

So why aren't we all experiencing the promises of God turned into actual provisions? If the promises are real enough, could there be something else wrong? We must acknowledge there is "something else." In our search for the culprit, we are usually required to turn the searchlight on ourselves. It isn't that we need to pray more, give more time to Bible study, go to more prayer meetings, try harder to "be good" or give more money to missions. All of these things are profitable, but they aren't at the heart of this particular problem.

Between us and the fulfillment of God's beautiful

promises always lies a situation containing temptation—and it is how we respond to temptation that determines whether or not we receive the fulfillment of our promise.

The Greek word that we translate as *temptation* in the Bible means "that which puts us to the proof—whether by good or evil design." Temptation is designed to bring out what is really in our hearts. This reveals what we really are!

For example, steel must be tempered by heat and put to the test under varying degrees of stress to see how it will react for its intended use. Temptation puts to the test how we will react in a situation related to the promise God has given us. If we react according to biblical specifications, the provision will be ours. It is not earned or deserved—because God's gifts are always free; but the question is whether or not we have the capacity to receive what God has promised.

Untempered steel, given too much pressure, will break. Fulfillment of a promise, without preparation, can break us as well. Can you see there is reason for temptation? Its purpose is not to make life hard or difficult but to assist in the preparation needed to receive the good things God desires to give.

Seen in this perspective, temptation isn't something frightening or to be avoided. Rather it is a necessary part of our Christian lives—something we should understand and face eagerly and joyfully. After all, temptation is designed to prepare us to receive what we long to have.

The Bible is our textbook. We will find as we search its pages that the purpose and principle of temptation are clearly revealed and demonstrated here—beginning with the Old Testament and carrying on through the New

Testament. A series of test cases will show how temptation provided the turning point which determined the success or failure of experiencing fulfilled promises.

The Christian life can never be defined in methods. We can never discover a formula for how to face temptation and thus receive the fulfillment of God's promises. However, we will discover that God always operates according to clearly defined principles. When we understand these principles and learn how to apply them in our lives, we can move on and grow up into the fullness of life as the Bible presents it.

Right now—before we go any further—why not ask God to open your own understanding to this exciting possibility and say with me, "Lord, teach me Thy ways."

chapter two

Conditional Promises

Between us and the fulfillment of each of God's promises stands a situation that includes temptation. Let's take a closer look at some of the basic promises God offers all who come to Him and see at what point—in relation to the promise—temptation enters the picture.

Nothing is sadder, in my opinion, than Christians who have resigned themselves to the erroneous idea that God either cannot or will not pour out His blessing on us today. To hear some Christians talk, you would think God a tight-fisted miser who only dribbles out enough blessings to keep us going in this present world; or that He is unfair, raining riches on some and not on others— healing some and not others—according to His inscrutable whim.

The Bible pictures God as eager and anxious to give good things without preference or partiality. While the

Bible is often referred to as a Book of Promises, it is just as much a textbook that could be called *How to Turn Promises Into Provisions*. No promise in the entire Bible is an empty promise. Luke 1:37 tells us, "For with God nothing is ever impossible, and no word from God shall be without power or impossible of fulfillment" (Amplified).

The Children of Israel

Our first test case is the Israelites, God's chosen people. He brought them out of Egyptian slavery in order to bring them into a land flowing with milk and honey. His promise was,

> You may multiply greatly...in a land flowing with milk and honey....Then it shall come about when the Lord your God brings you into the land which He swore to your fathers...to give you great and splendid cities which you did not build, and houses full of all good things which you did not fill, and hewn cisterns which you did not dig, vineyards and olive trees which you did not plant (Deut. 6:3,10,11).

Remember, although we are speaking of a specific people in a certain place and time in history, the same promises are applicable to us today—as spiritual Israelites. God desires to bring us out of whatever bondage we may be in—psychological, spiritual or physical—in order to bring us into "a land flowing with milk and honey." This is a picture of the abundance of good things (both spiritual and physical) that He has for us in this life.

It sounds almost too good to be true, doesn't it? God wants to give us everything we could possibly need—things for which we are not required to labor! Moses goes on to say to the Israelites, "God will drive your enemies out before you" (see v. 19).

In plain, everyday language, this means that God desires to lead us into a situation—spiritual and physical—where He will provide for our every need— job, home, friends, clothes, food, peace of mind— everything our hearts may desire. To get all of this we do not have to work for it, earn it or deserve it.

If it is all that simple, why didn't the Israelites move on into the Promised Land? Instead, they wandered in the wilderness for forty years—grumbling and complaining all the way. The entire first generation of ex-slaves (with two notable exceptions, Joshua and Caleb) died in the wilderness before their children were able to enter the land.

Also—if it is all that simple—why aren't you and I dwelling in our own promised land right now? Instead, we may be wandering around in our own private wildernesses, probably doing our share of grumbling and complaining! And some of us are even likely to die there, without ever coming into the good life God has promised to us.

First of all, let us take another look at the promise made to the Israelites. We quite often make the common mistake that these people seem to have made— that of lifting the promise out of its surrounding and supporting framework. Reading Deuteronomy again, we see:

> If you obey these commands you will become a great nation in a glorious land "flowing with milk and honey," even as the God of your fathers promised you....Listen: Jehovah is our God, Jehovah alone. You must love him with all your

heart, soul, and might. And you must think constantly about these commandments I am giving you today. You must teach them to your children and talk about them when you are at home or out for a walk; at bedtime and the first thing in the morning....When the Lord your God has brought you into the land he promised your ancestors... when he has given you great cities full of good things—cities you didn't build, wells you didn't dig, and vineyards and olive trees you didn't plant—and when you have eaten until you can hold no more, then beware lest you forget the Lord who brought you out of...slavery. When you are full, don't forget to be reverent to him and to serve him and to use his name alone to endorse your promises....You must not provoke him and try his patience [The King James Version says: Ye shall not tempt the Lord your God]....If you obey him, all will go well for you, and you will be able to go in and possess the good land which the Lord promised....You will also be able to throw out all the enemies living in your land, as the Lord agreed to help you do (Deut. 6:3-19, TLB).

The promises sound a little different when they are placed in the right context, don't they? Listen to another promise made in Isaiah 1:19: "If ye be willing and obedient, ye shall eat of the good of the land" (KJV).

What is God saying? Do you notice some *if* openings in these statements? In the case of Moses' reminding the Israelites of God's promises, he speaks of "obey these commands." These are the commandments given to Moses by God—the Ten Commandments. We might capsule his admonition and say, "Obey the commandments, love God with all your heart, soul and might, teach this to your children, and when you come into the good land and have eaten your fill, don't forget who gave it all to you; don't provoke or tempt God. Obey Him and He will chase out your enemies before you so that you can possess the land. Be willing and obedient, and you may eat of the good of the land. You will prosper and be rich.''

How do we reconcile these two thoughts? On one hand God says He wants to give us good things which we do not have to earn or we do not deserve. On the other hand, He says we can't have the good provisions *unless* we do certain things. Is this consistent? Even more important, is it consistent with the New Testament which tells us that God gave His only Son, Jesus Christ, as a free gift—and that by accepting Him as our Savior we no longer have to pay for our own sins with the death penalty? Instead of a death penalty, we are told we can receive the gift of God's grace, His pardon and eternal life in Christ.

A Hot Debate

This brings us to what is probably one of the most debated aspects of the Christian life: legalism versus ''everything by grace.'' There are groups of believers on both sides of the fence—those who lean to the legalistic by overemphasizing the belief that we must observe certain rules and regulations in order to be in right standing with God and those who say that under the New Covenant (the covenant sealed by Jesus Christ on the cross), we cannot earn God's gifts by keeping rules and regulations. All things are free in Christ.

Must we choose up sides and come out fighting? God forbid! Neither extreme position is correct. Both have caught some aspect of the truth and carried it too far. Error may come by emphasis or neglect. God doesn't want legalism but neither does He want disobedience! In reality, everything God has for us is a gift. We cannot earn anything by our own goodness or efforts; however, God's gifts can be received only on certain conditions.

Just in case this sounds like double-talk to you, we shall look at some promises in the New Testament.

"If you abide in Me and My words abide in you, ask whatever you wish, and it shall be done for you" (John 15:7). This is Jesus Himself speaking, and He is giving a remarkable promise. But notice the *if*; there is a condition to the promise. In fact, I don't know of a single promise in the Bible that does not have a condition attached to it.

Consider the promise of salvation: "For God so loved the world, that He gave His only begotten Son, that whoever believes in Him should not perish, but have eternal life" (John 3:16). Some people are perishing because they haven't met the condition for salvation, which is offered as a free gift, only to those who choose to believe. The Amplified Bible explains the term *believing* as "anyone who trusts, clings to, relies on Jesus Christ." We are talking about more than lip service here; rather it is a matter of a total personal trust and reliance on Christ in every aspect of life. That is the condition.

The Conditions

The condition always describes *how* a promise is to be fulfilled. Only under these prescribed conditions can the promise become reality. Taking another promise of Jesus, we note: "I am the vine, you are the branches;

he who abides in Me, and I in him, he bears much fruit"
(John 15:5). The promise is that we shall produce fruit,
provided we live in Him and allow Him to live in us.
Jesus goes on to explain why this is so. "For apart from
Me you can do nothing. If anyone does not abide in Me,
he is thrown away as a branch, and dries up; and they
gather them, and cast them into the fire, and they are
burned" (vv. 5,6). The reason the condition is necessary
is a very simple one: apart from Jesus Christ we cannot produce spiritual fruit!

The reasons for putting conditions on the promises
given to the Israelites were the same: apart from God
they would not be able to possess the land and enjoy
the kind of life God wanted for them. Can you see that
giving the condition, "If you are willing and obedient,"
before the promise, "you will eat of the good of the
land," was because of the fact that God knew if they
tried to do it in their own way, they would fail miserably
in the end? Their obedience to God was designed to
reduce their dependency on their own resources and
strength and increase their dependency on God.

God is not a tyrant who wants us all to cower in obedience before Him; He loves us and knows our natures
well enough to see that—left to our own devices—we
always make a mess of things. When Jesus said, "On
your own, apart from Me, you can do nothing," He
meant that apart from Him we cannot do anything truly
worthwhile and lasting. We just cannot produce the kind
of fruits He can produce in us and through us when we
stay close to Him and depend on Him. We need to give
up our self-sufficiency so that we can come to a place
in our Christian experience where we cease from our
own frantic labor and let Him do the work.

Greater Works

Another truth Jesus tried to impress on His disciples was that if they believed in Him, they would one day do greater works than He was doing. One day the disciples asked Jesus, "What are we to do that we may [habitually] be working the works of God?—What are we to do to carry out what God requires? Jesus replied, This is the work (service) that God asks of you: that you believe in the One Whom He has sent—that you cleave to, trust, rely on and have faith in His Messenger" (John 6:28,29, Amplified). Jesus said that when we stop trying to do things in our own strength and recognize our own insufficiency, then we can let Him work through us.

As Christians, we know in our hearts that what we do in our own strength "for the Lord" amounts to zero. We may busy ourselves building churches, organizing missions, revivals, Sunday school rallies. But *we* cannot save anyone. We cannot heal anybody. We cannot comfort the brokenhearted, give sight to the blind or set anybody free from a prison of guilt. It is only when we come to a position of total reliance on Jesus—total trust, obedience and rest from our own labors—that we will see Jesus bring salvation to others through us; see Him heal and comfort others and set them free through us. Always it is His doing through our willingness and obedience to His command.

The Promise

This is the *only* way we can ever enter our promised land. Because the promised land is a place of rest, frantic self-efforts do not belong there. Hebrews describes God's promise about a place of rest and how we may enter:

Let us fear lest, while a promise remains of entering His rest, any one of you should seem to have
come short of it. For indeed we have had good
news preached to us, just as they also, but the word
they heard did not profit them, because it was not
united by faith in those who heard. For we who
have believed enter that rest....For if Joshua had
given them rest, He would not have spoken of
another day after that. There remains therefore a
Sabbath rest for the people of God....Let us
therefore be diligent to enter that rest, lest anyone
fall through following the same example of disobedience (Heb. 4:1-3,8,9,11).

Some people may teach that this place of rest is where
we enter after death, but I do not find this consistent
with the teachings of Jesus. He said—over and over
again—that we are to cease from our own labors now,
letting Him work through us. Our promised land today
is a place of rest where we will dwell in cities we didn't
build and receive good things for which we did not
work—because God alone will do the work for and
through us. It is physically and spiritually impossible
for Him to do this until we surrender our attempt to do
it for ourselves.

The condition God gives us is that we must be willing to give up our own ways and work and be obedient
to His every command as He lives in and works through
us. God's promises must be seen in relation to their
conditions.

It is in the midst of our reaction to the conditions that
temptation enters the picture. *Temptation relates to the
promise through the condition.* When a promise is given
with a condition, God is saying, "I will do this if you

will do that." Temptation then presents us with the choice either to fulfill God's condition or to ignore it. If we fulfill the condition, we can enter into the provision—the promised land. If we ignore the condition, we will not be able to receive fulfillment of the promise.

Returning to Hebrews, we read words ascribed to the Holy Spirit:

> Therefore I was angry with this generation, and said, ''They always go astray in their heart; and they did not know My ways''; as I swore in My wrath, ''They shall not enter My rest'' (3:10,11).

God's promises are real; so are His conditions. There is still a promised land waiting for you and me. The decision to go there becomes an individual choice. Don't be afraid to venture out into God's provision—your promised land!

chapter three

The Wilderness Complex

Why does God place a "wilderness area" between us and our promised land? For the Israelites, it was a geographical fact that the wilderness existed between the Red Sea and Canaan, their Promised Land. They could not get to Canaan except through the wilderness. For us, the wilderness is not a geographical fact; nevertheless, it is there—a very real wilderness! Between the promise and its actual fulfillment lies a physical and spiritual wilderness, consisting of problems, difficulties and confusion. This is, of course, the area where temptation enters.

We have seen that temptation relates to the promise through the condition. It is in the wilderness that we come to the point of questioning the validity of the condition, and at times the promise itself. That kind of question must be solved before we can move on into the provision—and God placed the wilderness experience in our way to bring about that confrontation. We must come to see the validity of His conditions and fulfill them before we can move on.

This may sound extremely serious and definite to some of us who like to think that God's love is of such a nature that He won't hold back the fulfillment of a promise just because the condition isn't completely met. We may ask, "Didn't Jesus take care of all that when He died for us? Didn't Jesus pay our debt and fulfill our conditions so that all we have to do is ask and receive? If we love Him and say our prayers, He will surely give us the promises we have claimed and hung onto for all these years."

If this has been your thinking, you may be in danger of making a serious mistake. The promises you are waiting for may never become yours. I am convinced that if it were at all possible, God would unconditionally give us everything for which we ask. But He cannot, because if He did, it would destroy us. Being a father I have known the delight of seeing my children walk in the principles so that I can give to them. But I knew that giving them something for which they weren't qualified was destructive.

John D. Rockefeller once said, in essence: "I have seldom, if ever, found a place where I could give in substantial amounts without hurting people." If John D. Rockefeller felt like that, how do you think God feels?

Lord, I'm Ready

When I first read God's promise of the land flowing with milk and honey—the land with wells, vineyards, cities that I need not labor for, a land just waiting for me—I said, "Lord, that is just wonderful! I'm willing and obedient and ready for it!''

Then, in a way God often speaks to me, my impression was, ''No, son, you're not!''

My reply was, ''Why not?''

And His answer came, ''Son, the one thing you cannot stand right now is success.''

But I argued, ''Why, Lord! Me? *I can* stand it. Give me my inheritance right now.''

To which the Lord asked, ''You mean like the prodigal son?''

How did the prodigal son get into trouble? By demanding his inheritance too soon! When all that money was in his pocket, he forgot about his father. Too much too soon nearly destroyed him, and it will do the same to us. (See Prov. 20:21, Amplified.)

Have you ever watched an instant movie star be "born"? Overnight she is chosen by the star makers, given the Madison-Avenue treatment, television, magazines, parties, attention and admiration. Soon she becomes a self-willed and self-centered individual. Before long, she is so conceited no one can work with her. Like a shooting star falling from the sky, she shines brilliantly for a season and is burned up, cast away and forgotten. This may be an extreme example, but watch the pattern in any area where someone comes into sudden success or riches. A million-dollar inheritance can destroy a person who is immature and unprepared. You don't place your son as head of your business when he's 15; you give him a job as clean-up boy, and, as he proves himself capable, you give him more responsibility.

This is true with material possessions and with spiritual riches, as well. Our heavenly Father wants us to become spiritually mature individuals. He wants us to be His witnesses in all the world. He wants to preach powerful sermons through us—do miracles—to show His power and love through us. He cannot, however, dump the whole package on us before we are mature enough to handle the responsibility.

What do you think would happen to me if a wealthy man said, "Mumford, I think you're the greatest teacher I have ever heard. You are doing a marvelous work for the Lord. I'm going to send you $5,000 a month for the rest of your life, install you and your family in a new beachfront villa and give you a new chauffeur-driven Cadillac every year."

I can tell you what would happen, because I know my heart. I would start thinking, My, I'm really quite a guy; God is pretty lucky to have me around. I would soon forget that God is the source of everything I am and have, and I'd start thinking *I* was the reason things were going so well.

A Warning

Moses warned the Israelites about four things that could happen when they had received riches and eaten until they were full. Do these have relevance for us today?

1. They could easily forget God.

2. They could attribute their good life to a source other than God.

3. They could provoke God by trying His patience.

4. They could test and tempt Him.

It is a fairly simple matter to see how one could easily forget God or attribute success to a source other than God when success and riches come our way. A businessman who makes it to the top of his profession, or a politician who wins a landslide election, can be tempted to think it all happened because he did a good job or was a great man.

But how do we provoke God? The Israelites did it by asking for more than God wanted them to have at the moment. They wanted a sign greater than He was pleased to give. This is a temptation that we are also faced with when things prosper for us.

Young Christians, excited over their newfound faith and convinced that God can and will do anything they ask, often go around looking for a situation where they can demonstrate the power of God to others.

This happened to me. During my first year in Bible college, I began to understand a little of the Scriptures concerning divine healing. I was convinced that God could heal anyone—anytime! Once on a student-minister assignment to a church near the college, I found myself face to face with a man in a wheelchair. He had been sick for many years. Eager to see God's power manifested, I stepped over to the man, commanding in a strong voice, "In the name of Jesus, be healed and stand up!" Nothing happened. I was crushed, of course; and the man, whose hopes had soared for an instant, felt his faith shaken.

In my immaturity I had rushed ahead, asking for a miracle, a sign that God had in no way indicated He wanted to perform right then and there. God can heal. I have seen His healing power at work in many instances. But at that particular time I had fallen for the temptation to test God. Had He healed the man at that time, not because of my faithfulness and obedience but because He desired to heal him, I probably would have swelled in pride over my "spirituality," seeing myself as MUMFORD—THE MIRACLE MAN. I would have been in far greater danger of destroying myself and others than before the incident.

When those who receive riches—material or spiritual—consequently stumble and fall, it isn't because the riches in themselves are dangerous or destructive, but because those who receive them are not prepared to handle them.

A ten-speed bike is a wonderful gift and so is an electric handsaw. Have you ever seen a youngster go over a curb on his new ten-speed, getting badly bruised, or heard of a fellow who cut off his finger with his new power saw? Have you seen a family come into sudden prosperity and shortly thereafter their children run wild on new motorbikes and get failing grades in school, the marriage goes on the rocks and the wife runs off with another man? What is your reaction?

You could say, "Ten-speeds and electric power saws are dangerous; I'll never have any. Prosperity leads to misery. I hope I never get rich." Or, "I can see it takes skill to operate a ten-speed and an electric power saw. I better learn how to handle such things before I get one. Prosperity must be handled carefully. I better start learning responsible stewardship so that I am prepared if God wants to trust me with more possessions in life."

Fear of Success

The first reaction—"I'll never ride a ten-speed"—springs from something I call the *wilderness complex*. We have watched others get hurt by a measure of success, and so we think we are safer while we're poor and in need. When I first saw some of my contemporaries rise to fame and position in the church and later fail, I developed a full-grown wilderness complex. I honestly feared success and was afraid that if it came to me I would forget God, get big-headed and stumble. "Lord, just keep me broke and humble, half-sick and driving an old car so that I'll stay dependent on You— and faithful. But don't bless me, Lord. I know I couldn't stand it!"

The Israelites experienced wonderful miracles from God, ate their fill and promptly forgot God—or tried His patience by asking for more. Over and over again they repeated the same pattern. Consequently, their wilderness wanderings were a series of problems with no satisfactory solutions. We see some disastrous consequences come to our contemporary wilderness wanderers and conclude that we don't want any blessings. We decide we'd rather stay in a condition of continuous need so that we won't forget our constant dependency on God.

As a part of the wilderness complex, we have developed the idea that success always spoils, power always corrupts, riches are the root of evil. We've become so used to dwelling in the wilderness that we think God wants us to remain there permanently. We accept the wilderness as the only normal way of life for a spiritual Christian.

We reason: Jesus was poor and rode into Jerusalem on a borrowed donkey. So we say it is Christlike to be poor. We extend that thought even further and say it is Christlike and spiritual to suffer constant duress, sickness, financial problems, persecutions and hardships. We say we can best glorify God by going through these difficulties in order for others to see our patience and conclude that God enables us to bear our burdens without complaining. Permanent wilderness dwellers look critically at those who appear to live happily in a life free from obvious problems and say, "Just wait—God will deal with you and you will come to understand the serious reality of this life in our sin-sick world. Suffering will come to you, too. Then you will understand what it is all about and become really spiritual like the rest of us who are called upon to suffer."

This is a form of self-imposed martyrdom that serves to keep you just as far removed from the fulfillment of God's promises as if you were outwardly rebellious and arrogantly disobedient to God's commands. To take pride in suffering and poverty is just as disastrous as taking pride in accumulated riches or a high position.

Can you see that those Christians who measure their spirituality by their humble station in life are just as much in error as those who say that God always goes first class? The latter measure their spirituality by how much God provides for them. This tendency is called *success ethics*. The two extremes—the wilderness complex and those who run in the prosperity pack—are both reacting. Spirituality, or closeness to God, cannot be measured by either the presence or absence of material and spiritual blessings.

I once had a friend who sincerely wanted to serve God as a missionary to the poorest of Indians. For years he lived in very poor circumstances, giving away everything he received. But instead of sending him to the mission field where he could continue to live in abject poverty, God sent this man to a very prosperous church in a wealthy suburb. There he had to minister to the champagne-and-jet-set crowd. My friend was deeply disturbed about the situation. He didn't consider it proper to serve God in such luxurious surroundings. He found himself unable to cope with the turn of events until God impressed upon him: "For many years you have been more than willing to adjust your standard of living down to suffer with the poor. Now I am asking you to adjust your standard of living up, so that you can be My messenger to these people in a way they can understand and accept."

God wants to bring us to a place where we can be willing and obedient on a full stomach, as well as on an empty one. Paul learned this lesson and passes it on to us in Philippians 4:12,13:

I know how to get along with humble means, and I also know how to live in prosperity; in any and every circumstance I have learned the secret of being filled and going hungry, both of having abundance and suffering need. I can do all things through Him who strengthens me.

Keep Walking

Most of us know more about being dependent on God when we have nothing than when we have a great deal. We have more experience dwelling in the wilderness than tasting of the good of the promised land. While the wilderness is a necessary experience in our Christian lives, we were never meant to be permanent residents there. We must go through the wilderness because we need to learn dependence on God. When we learn genuine dependence on Him, and when we stop forgetting Him as soon as things run smoothly for a while, we don't need the reminders of the wilderness any longer. We then have an open invitation to enter the land God has waiting for us.

We may receive the fullness of His promise in one area of our lives and go through a wilderness experience in another area. There is a vast difference between genuine wilderness *experience* and a wilderness *complex*. Judy and I went through a wilderness experience in the area of finances while I was in Bible college.

When I first began to trust that God would supply my financial needs, I prayed, "Lord, I depend on You for my finances." Almost immediately the Lord began supplying financial help from people who sent it through the mail. I said, "Thank You, Lord. You are providing in a wonderful way." Then came a period of two months when, although I looked expectantly into my mailbox every day, it was always empty! I became very upset and wondered what was the matter with God. Finally I realized that I had shifted my dependency from God to the mailbox. God knew my heart and stopped the money through the mail so that I could get back my perspective and realize who was the real source of my supply. I learned that God can supply in any way He chooses, but He wants me not to become dependent on the provision—but on Him.

As we learn to depend on God for finances, finances are no longer a problem, whether one is a millionaire or living happily on an income of $150 a week. Dependency on God must be more than lip service!

God desires to bring us into the promised land in every area of our lives. This was His plan for the Israelites, and it is His plan for us. He wants to provide for us— keep us in health, out of debt, united and strong as families and filled with joy, peace and love. He wants to bless us in order that others may see His goodness and, in turn, come to Him to be blessed.

God's original plan for the Israelites was that they might be an example to their day and world of His goodness and His ability to undertake in their behalf.

They were chosen so that they might be instruments in His hands in drawing the entire world to Himself. Today we are His chosen people. God doesn't want us wandering around in the wilderness years on end. He wants to bless and undertake for us in order that we may be an example to our confused and needy world. He wants our lives, homes, children to reflect His glory so that those who do not know Him will be drawn to Him.

When people come to us, as individuals, or to our church doors, God doesn't want them to turn sadly away because our lives are shallow and empty—no different from the lives they seek so desperately to escape. He wants Christians to be noticeably different—not because they talk Christianity, but because our lives are radiant with a joy and power which only Christ can give. If our lives—at church, home, in the neighborhood, at work—were like that, then the tired, sick, desperate, the rebels and doubters would all come to us seeking and finding answers.

Jeremiah wrote about this deep desire on God's part:
And I will cleanse them from all their iniquity by which they have sinned against Me, and I will pardon all their iniquities by which they have sinned against Me, and by which they have transgressed against Me. And it shall be to Me a name of joy, praise, and glory before all the nations of the earth, which shall hear of all the good that I do for them, and they shall fear and tremble because of all the good and all the peace that I make for it (Jer. 33:8,9).
Jesus expressed His Father's desire this way:
You are the light of the world. A city set on a hill

cannot be hidden....Let your light shine before men in such a way that they may see your good works, and glorify your Father who is in heaven (Matt. 5:14,16).

God wants to restore our lives and cleanse every bit of rebellion from our hearts. His desire is that our lives be a source of praise and glory to His goodness. When this is accomplished, we can move from the wilderness into the promised land and be the fulfillment of Jesus' commands to be a light in our world to God's glory.

Remember, we were never meant to be permanent wilderness dwellers. We are to learn *how* to walk through the wilderness into His provision.

chapter four

The Law of the Four Ps

C hristianity is not complicated. The relationship between God and humanity can be understood in terms simple enough for a child to grasp. Yet the spiritual implications of these truths bring the wisest to a point of awe.

Christianity in operation is not only practical but it is also completely dependable. In His dealing with us, God gives a straightforward conditional statement: "If you will do this, I will do that; on the other hand, if you refuse, this will happen." In theology, this is called an *objective propositional revelation*. God gives us a proposition; if we follow it, the outcome will be just as He promised.

We have seen that God always makes a conditional promise, followed by a problem situation where temptation will provoke a decision either to fulfill God's condition or ignore it. The fulfillment of the promise (or the provision) cannot come until after we have made the decision—and then only if we decide to obey God's Word.

I have found this pattern to be absolutely invariable in God's workings with us. (See biblical examples in Appendix.) It is consistent throughout the Bible as well as in my personal experience. I have never found an exception to this rule. An easy way to remember the pattern is to think of it as "The Law of the Four Ps."

God gives us a *promise*, which is linked to a *principle* (or condition), followed by a *problem* (temptation in the wilderness)—leading to a *provision*!

Understanding the workings of this law, we would then realize that unfulfilled promises should not be the normal Christian experience. The promises are meant to be fulfilled. The trouble is, most of us bog down in the problem because we don't understand it as part of God's pattern. I used to think that if I prayed to receive a promise and then stumbled into a problem, it meant my prayer was not going to be answered. Somehow I had received a problem instead of a provision. But, according to the Law of the Four Ps, the problem doesn't come *instead of* but *as part of* or *as a means of* obtaining the provision.

Many Christians find it difficult to understand how God would use a problem as part of His plan to bring us into the provision. We want to blame the problem on the devil and think he interfered and upset God's intention. There is no question but that the devil is in the picture—but he is only there with God's permission. We need the problem to prepare for God's provision. James saw this principle and wrote: "Blessed is the man who shall endure temptation: for when he is tried, he shall receive..." (James 1:12, KJV).

In my early understanding, I thought that when I had prayed for a fish, somehow God by mistake had given me a serpent. I wanted a promise but stumbled into a problem. Gradually I came to understand that that which appeared to be a serpent was actually a fish. My job was to hold onto God's promise (if you ask for a fish He will not give you a serpent) while I work through the problem (it looks and acts like a serpent). Suddenly, to my amazement, the problem ceases and I'm left in possession of a fish which is the provision. All of this hinges on the principle of what God has said!

The Bible contains innumerable cases where we can observe the Law of the Four Ps at work. They are put there to teach us to expect this same pattern in our own lives. Once we claim a promise, we should make certain we understand the principle of *how* to turn our promise into provision. Then we should expect some sort of situation where we will be tempted to ignore God's Word. If we decide to ignore His Word, there cannot be a provision. If we decide to fulfill the condition or the principle, we can confidently expect God to bring us into the provision.

The pitfall at this point is that we are apt to be caught unaware when the problem arises. We seldom see the connection between it and the promise. Therefore, we are likely to become discouraged and fail. Expecting the problem keeps us prepared, and once we recognize the wilderness situation, we can usually go through it with less pain and in a shorter period of time.

The Old Testament Speaks

We shall use the wilderness journey of the Israelites as our prime test case. The writers of the New Testament used this same experience as a pattern for all believers because the promises God established for them are offered to us, as well, through the Person of Jesus Christ. The Israelites received their promise in Egypt when God said, ''I will lead you to a wonderful land flowing with milk and honey.'' When we accepted Jesus Christ as Savior, we became eligible for the same promise: ''I will lead you into a place of abundant blessings.''

Our map shows us that God brought the children of Israel to Mount Sinai and gave them the principles—the Ten Commandments—and the condition—''If you are willing and obedient, you will eat of the good of the land.'' Then came the wilderness, or the problem.

And why did God provide this wilderness experience? For the same reason a temptation experience is necessary

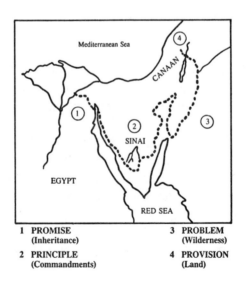

| 1 | PROMISE (Inheritance) | 3 | PROBLEM (Wilderness) |
| 2 | PRINCIPLE (Commandments) | 4 | PROVISION (Land) |

for us today. We need to learn who we are and who

God is in a way we will never forget. Thus, we can safely come into our provision without becoming haughty, proud and consequently destroying ourselves. Listen as Moses speaks for God:

> Remember all the way which the Lord your God has led you in the wilderness these forty years, that He might humble you, testing you, to know what was in your heart, whether you would keep His commandments or not....Beware...lest, when you have eaten and are satisfied, and have built good houses and lived in them, and when your herds and your flocks multiply, ...then your heart becomes proud, and you forget the Lord your God who brought you out from the land of Egypt (Deut. 8:2,11-14).

The purpose of the wilderness is always to make us recognize our own insufficiency and God's all-sufficiency. Once we realize this, willingness and obedience follow. When I recognize that I cannot do something on my own, I should be willing to give up trying to do it in my own strength and be obedient to the command of God who *can* get it done.

Salvation

God's gift of salvation is subject to the Law of the Four Ps, too.

To the sinner who seeks assurance that he or she has indeed been accepted by Christ and forgiven of sins, the four Ps come into play. Promise: If you receive and believe on My Son, you will be saved (John 3:16). Principle: Those who believe, adhere to and rely on Jesus Christ can know they are saved and have assurance that they are children of God. Problem: "I've been too great a sinner. I don't feel saved. There are too many hypocrites. The voices I hear say I will never be saved because of that abortion...." The storm rages; the problem is real.

Somewhere between the promise, principle and provision lies a wilderness area where we will be beset with doubts and the temptation to disbelieve God's Word. Some of us are prepared for doubts in this area. Evangelists and evangelical organizations circulate booklets advising new Christians to memorize God's promises of salvation. They know these scriptures will be needed to combat the doubts. Salvation is based on: "God said it; I believe it; that settles it in my heart." This is good advice. Feelings are dangerous and false indicators of what is really true. We all know that we can be saved without feeling saved. So we learn to stand on God's Word, choosing to believe Him rather than our feelings. This is the essence of faith—believing what God has said, regardless of what our senses or the circumstances seem to indicate.

Today multitudes of Christians are struggling in their first wilderness of doubts about forgiveness of sins. They come to the altar again and again saying, "I just don't know. Maybe I better ask God to save me again." They have never fully understood the principle and they are totally unprepared for the problem. There is no way to get to the provision of real peace in God except through the problem of doubt. You must come to the point of deciding—in spite of some convincing factors of feelings and rational doubts—that God's Word is to be trusted. You must choose to believe that Christ is indeed God's Son who died for your personal rebellion and sins. You will never be convinced or have peace with God any other way. No overwhelming proof will come your way before you make your decision. The peace and assurance can only come after you have decided to trust God's Word in the midst of uncertainty. That is faith.

Acquaint yourself with God's Word on the matter. God's part is already an established fact, done and sealed by Christ on the cross.

The condition left up to us is that we turn from our efforts at saving ourselves, admit our rebellion (sin), accept Christ as our Savior as well as our Lord and Master. This makes us eligible for another promise: Those who believe in Christ will receive power to become the children of God (see John 1:12). If we do our part of the condition (cling to, rely on, trust and believe in Jesus Christ), we can be absolutely certain that God has done His. We have His Word on it. But we can also be certain that our sense of security and peace in God can only come after a period of serious doubt and questioning.

Healing

Healing is another gift subject to the Law of the Four Ps. A man once asked me, "If you can't get healed when you ask for it, how do you know you are saved when you ask for it?" I wrestled with this question for some time before having an adequate answer.

If we were taught the principle of healing as thoroughly as we are taught the principle of salvation, we would be able to hold on to our healing. I do not mean to imply that healing is as universal a promise as salvation. The Bible tells us that all who call on the name of Jesus Christ shall be saved. The same universal promise does not apply to healing, because illness, aging and physical death are part of our world. The Bible does not promise that our sick world will be completely healed before Christ returns.

However, God *does* promise to heal; and when that promise is given to an individual, the fulfillment is meant to be received. In that case, I believe if the promise of healing is accepted in the same way that we accept our promise of salvation, we will be able to lay claim to the promise of healing in spite of doubts, feelings and recurring symptoms.

Refusing to believe that God puts a problem between you and the provision does not change this reality. It is increasingly clear to me that certain groups seem to be able to take the promise, understand the principle, work through the problem and receive the provision in specific areas that others cannot. I've seen this happen in the area of physical healing, financial provision, strong marriage or effective evangelism. How badly we as the body of Christ need to cease from strife and learn from one another.

One remarkable illustration of this point strikes me. Some years ago, sitting on a platform in a rather large church, I noticed that very few of the people in the congregation wore eye glasses. Upon inquiry, I discovered that the pastor had been healed of bad eyes. He knew the promise, preached the principle, faced the problem and had brought many of his people through to physical healing of their eyesight. The application is obvious.

I am convinced that God intends for Christians to enjoy greater health and a higher percentage of healings than we see evidenced in our churches today. It is safer to expound on Paul's "thorn in the flesh" (2 Cor. 12:7) than to risk teaching on healing. There is a serious discrepancy between what God has made available to us in Christ and what we are actually experiencing. In a large measure, this is due to the fact that most of us consider our feelings as the only reliable gauge for whether or not we are physically well. If healing follows the Law of the Four Ps, we should expect the problem to contain physical symptoms designed to test our faith in God's promise.

A woman was dying slowly of multiple sclerosis. She believed that God would heal her and many people had prayed for her. Still she continued to get worse. She kept on pleading with God and told her friends she thought He would answer her prayers soon. However, the time came when she was placed in a hospital, and she lost her eyesight and ability to move her limbs. The doctors feared she had only a day or two more to live.

One of her friends visited her and leaning over her bedside said, "Stop waiting for God to heal you soon. Accept the fact that He has healed you already. Thank Him for it and stop thinking about how sick you feel." It was as if a bright light had gone on in the dying woman's mind. She suddenly understood why she was feeling worse all the time. She had been keeping her mind on her feelings instead of on Christ's finished work. She began to thank God, and, within hours, her body responded. In a few days, she was home from the hospital and back on her feet. When she tells her story, she remarks that if she had stayed in bed waiting for God to heal her instead of accepting that He had already done it, she would have been dead in spite of God's provision waiting for her.

The Israelites died in the wilderness in spite of God's provision of a Promised Land because they could never accept the problem as part of God's plan. Many who could be healed are not—because they do not understand how to go through the problem into the provision of health. In that particular wilderness, you will be faced with the choice to believe either God's Word that He has healed you or your own sense and feeling that you are still sick.

The many healings recorded in the Bible are all different, but there is one common denominator throughout: faith. Faith, we know, is the determination to believe, trust in and rely on God's Word over and above what our senses or circumstances may tell us. Faith alone can take us through the problem into the provision.

Fruit of the Spirit

The Bible tells us that the characteristics of a normal Christian life should be an abundance of love, joy, peace, patience, kindness, goodness, faithfulness, gentleness and self-control. But these Christian qualities are provided for us in promise form and can become translated into real experience only through the workings of the Law of the Four Ps. In Galatians 5:22,23, the principle and the promise are given: "When the Holy Spirit controls our lives he will produce this kind of fruit in us: love, joy, peace, patience, kindness, goodness, faithfulness, gentleness and self-control" (TLB).

Do you see the condition: that the Holy Spirit must control our lives? He must produce the fruit. They cannot be produced by willpower; they grow only when we are rightly connected to Christ through the Holy Spirit. Between the promise, principle and the provision, we expect a problem. In this case, it is a wilderness situation where the fruit of the Spirit will either be given an opportunity to grow—or be crushed by our self-will.

In John 15:1-4, Jesus describes how fruit is encouraged

to grow:

> I am the true vine, and My Father is the vine-dresser. Every branch in Me that does not bear fruit, He takes away; and every branch that bears fruit, He prunes it, that it may bear more fruit....As the branch cannot bear fruit of itself, unless it abides in the vine, so neither can you, unless you abide in Me.

The pruning back for greater strength and greater production is an apt description of a wilderness experience. Our real-life experience comes through circumstances in which we are squeezed to the point where we can't continue to act loving and patient in our own strength. We are forced to admit to our own unlovingness and impatience. We are forced to make a decision. We can either admit our insufficiency, confess our unlovingness and turn ourselves over to God, asking Him to make us loving or we can refuse to see God's hand in the problem, explode and blame the whole thing on the terrible circumstances we have fallen into.

When we pray for God to make us more loving, we can expect Him to put us into a problem situation where we are confronted with people who are difficult to love—so difficult that it is impossible for us to love them of ourselves. The provision—a new ability to love people—comes only as we go through the problem and allow Christ to take over and control our natural inclinations.

The fruit of the Spirit does not grow automatically in a Christian's life—only as one deliberately chooses to stick to God's principles through a problem situation.

Marriage

God gave wonderful promises concerning Christian

marriage. When Jesus was asked about marriage, He quoted from the Old Testament. God created male and female, and "for this cause a man shall leave his father and mother, and shall cleave to his wife; and the two shall become one flesh" (Matt. 19:5).

The promise is that God intended to make two different people, with two different personalities, into one harmonious union. God promises to do it, because He knows two human beings cannot join themselves together in perfect union in their own strength. Most couples start out very much in love, but God intended to remake their human love into something far more reliable, enduring, exciting and joyous than anything they could experience in their own strength.

Between that glorious promise and God's intended provision must necessarily come a wilderness of problems. The difficulties of the wilderness are designed to show us that our own resources are insufficient to make a satisfying marriage union. God wants to make our marriage in such a way that we can never claim credit for it. We have to recognize that He made our marriage—and He alone can maintain it.

God wants us to realize that our marriage cannot succeed simply because we feel we are so well suited to each other—so kind and understanding, so much in love. He wants us to know that our marriage can be gloriously happy only because God makes it possible. On our own, we would have made a terrible mess. Our personalities would clash—our interests differing—and we would be headed toward stormy seas.

No marriage—regardless of how much the couple is in love at the start—can come into the fullness of a mature, rich and permanent relationship without going through some difficult problems. Unfortunately, very few couples see their problems as part of God's plan to bring them into this fuller relationship. A majority remain in the wilderness—enduring a family life that, at best, is a shadow of the joy God promised. A growing number of Christian couples follow the custom of their non-Christian friends and neighbors; when things get too rough, they divorce. The marriage perishes in the wilderness.

When the Pharisees asked Jesus why Moses had permitted easy divorce, Jesus answered, "Because of your hardness of heart, Moses permitted you to divorce your wives; but from the beginning it has not been this way" (Matt. 19:8). So we see it is not God's original intent that any marriage end in divorce. If we understand His promise, learn His conditions and principles, learn to hold on to them through the inevitable problems—then we will come into provision. When God has made husband and wife one in joyous union, divorce will be an impossible thought.

If you have already spent time in a wilderness situation in your marriage, ask God to teach you the principles. Hang on to them through the difficult circumstances, and you will soon enter your promised land. Unfulfilled promises are not the normal Christian life— neither are unhappy marriages. God wants to transform them into abundant provision.

Having realized the necessity for the problem, we are now prepared to take a closer look at this vital area and discover some possibilities for moving into the abundant provision God wants us to receive.

chapter five

Alternatives in the Problem

The problem is the central part of our journey from promise to provision. Our behavior in the problem determines to what extent, how soon or even whether or not we'll come into our provision!

Returning to our test case (the Israelites and their problems) and comparing them with our own experiences, we can observe three basic alternatives facing us during the problem or wilderness.

1. *Another lap.* Our initial negative response to the problem leads to an extended stay in the wilderness. God provides a similar set of circumstances to give us a chance at another lap through the same problem.

2. *Bleached bones.* Repeated negative responses cause us to perish in the wilderness. This does not mean we lose our eternal salvation, rather our promised provision. This is illustrated in 1 Corinthians 3:15, "If any man's work is burned up, he shall suffer loss; but he

himself shall be saved, yet so as through fire.''

3. *Stand and enter.* If our response is positive and we choose to stand on God's principles through the problem, we are able to enter our provision with little delay.

As we examine each of these alternatives, let us remember the Law of the Four Ps, the very real possibility of falling prey to a wilderness complex, and the goodness and patience of our God.

Another Lap

When the Israelites entered their wilderness experience, they had just come across the Red Sea and had seen God take care of their enemies behind them. They had received their promise in Egypt and had learned the basic principle: If they would only trust God and obey Him, He would lead them safely through the wilderness ahead.

We know they believed in both promise and principle because we read in Exodus 15 that the entire nation sang a song of victory and praise to God.

The Israelites were confident that God would take care of them because they had just seen how He drowned an entire army in the Red Sea. Had their first problem in the wilderness been an army pursuing them across the desert, I think they would have continued their singing, expecting God to repeat His miracle.

I recognize myself in the Israelites. Many times I have praised God for something He has done in my life. Then I've turned around, expecting Him to do the same thing over again. I seek to anticipate *how* God is going to solve a problem, which causes me to fall flat on my face when God moves in *His* way.

Immediately after the singing and dancing, God led the former slaves into the wilderness of Shur where they were three days without water. Then they arrived at Marah and couldn't drink the water in the spring because it was bitter. God demonstrated the condition of their hearts by sending a problem different in kind from the one they had seen Him solve before. Did they or didn't they trust Him to provide for them?

They did not respond as He had hoped they would. They didn't say, "God parted the Red Sea before us. Surely He can turn bitter water into sweet water. We'll just praise Him and watch Him perform another miracle." Instead, they turned to Moses and demanded, "Must we die of thirst here?" Because of their negative response, they extended their stay in the wilderness. God brought about another set of circumstances, providing them with another opportunity to choose to trust Him. They had to take another lap.

We often anticipate that God will work in one way and are unaware that He is already at work in our problem—where we least expect Him to be! If you have a difficult boss, you may pray that God will take care of your enemy. You expect God either to take that mean boss away or turn him into a nice guy. Instead your boss seems to be harder than ever. Isn't God answering your prayer? Of course He is, but in a different way from how you expected. God is dealing with the real enemy— your own pride and unyielding ego. And He is permitting the boss to become more difficult so that you will turn to Him and ask Him to take your pride and unyielding spirit and make you yield to Him instead. When you do, you may find that your boss has become surprisingly kind and understanding overnight!

We almost always make the mistake of blaming our difficulties on our circumstances—expecting God to change them—when we should realize that our own attitude is causing the problem. God can change our circumstances instantly if He wants to. When He doesn't, it is because He wants to change something in us. The circumstances are there to bring about what needs to be changed.

The continuing story of the wilderness journey of the people of Israel is told not only in the book of Exodus, but also in Leviticus, Numbers and Deuteronomy. We pick up with their experiences at Elim. Here they camped among palm trees beside twelve springs of water. Once more God showed them He could provide. Next they were led into the Sin wilderness. Here they couldn't find anything to eat. We recognize they were back facing the same problem in a slightly different guise. Instead of bitter water, they now had lack of food.

If our first response to a problem is negative, God will meet our immediate demand and move us on, providing a similar set of circumstances to confront us with the same choice again: to trust Him and stand on His principles or to ignore His principles and complain. We may not even recognize the pattern for a while, but there will be continuing difficulties of a similar nature, slowly increasing in severity.

Now we find the Israelites complaining even more about the lack of food than they had complained about the water. Gone was the assurance they had received when God turned bitter water into sweet. But God was patient with His chosen people. That evening it rained quail and in the morning manna covered the desert. Again God had responded to their complaints, demonstrating His love and ability to provide.

The following lap around the mountain led to

Rephidim, where there was no water at all. Here they were back facing a situation very similar to the one they had seen God solve before. How would they react? Would they remember His miracles and confidently expect another? No, it was more complaints—this time almost to the point of wanting to stone Moses. But God led them to Mount Horeb...instructed Moses to beat on a rock with his rod. Water gushed out and Moses named the place Massah, meaning, "tempting Jehovah to slay us"; for it was here the people of Israel argued against God and tempted Him to slay them by saying, "Is Jehovah going to take care of us or not?"

The wilderness between Egypt and Canaan can be crossed on foot in less than two weeks, but it took the Israelites forty years! With each lap, each confrontation with the problem, they chose to complain instead of trust God. With each lap their bitterness grew and their rebellion hardened. They didn't wait when Moses went up on Mount Sinai, but built themselves a golden calf in direct disobedience to the command God had just given them. They murmured and complained all the way across the desert; when they finally arrived at the border of the Promised Land and saw that it was full of fortified cities and enemies—some of them even giants—they panicked.

Bleached Bones
Twelve spies went over the border to look at the land. Ten of them said the land couldn't be taken. The last two, Joshua and Caleb, remembered God's words and believed them. They wanted to go into their provision, but the people refused to follow. Ten times the Israelites had tried God's patience—and finally the laps gave out. Their hearts were hardened in rebellion and God lost

His patience with them.

Christianity is something more than repeated forgiveness every time we do wrong. It also has to do with willingness and obedience. If we harden our hearts in the wilderness, the second alternative will be our end: our bones will bleach; we will perish in the problem; we will never come into the fullness of provision.

Moses pleaded with God to pardon the sins and God answered:

I have pardoned them according to your word; but indeed, as I live, all the earth will be filled with the glory of the Lord. Surely all the men who have seen My glory and My signs, which I performed in Egypt and in the wilderness, yet have put Me to the test these ten times and have not listened to My voice, shall by no means see the land which I swore to their fathers, nor shall any of those who spurned Me see it (Num. 14:20-23).

God said He would forgive the people. They did not lose their salvation, but they lost the opportunity to receive the fulfillment of the promise. Their bones bleached in the wilderness. They perished physically, although they were actually in possession of the promise.

The bleached bones are a sad spectacle in the desert, but it becomes our alternative if we continually respond negatively to the problems confronting us on our many laps around the wilderness. There are bleached bones strewn across many a modern-day wilderness.

After continual resistance, there may come a point of no return in God's dealings with us. Listen to this turning point in our test case:

Then the ten spies who had incited the rebellion against Jehovah by striking fear into the hearts of the people were struck dead before the Lord. Of all the spies, only Joshua and Caleb remained alive. What sorrow there was throughout the camp when Moses reported God's words to the people! They were up early the next morning and started towards the Promised Land. "Here we are!" they said. "We realize that we have sinned, but now we are ready to go into the land the Lord has promised us." But Moses said, "It's too late. Now you are disobeying the Lord's orders to return to the wilderness. Don't go ahead with your plan or you will be crushed by your enemies, for the Lord is not with you" (Num. 14:36-42, TLB).

This is a fearful thought: God will forgive us our sins against Him, but unless we allow Him to prepare us— unless we accept fully His principles and His problems— He cannot bring us into the promised land. How tragic that Christians who know His promises may spend their lives wandering in the wilderness—unable ever to see those promises turned into provision. In the end— bleached bones!

Stand and Enter!

The third alternative, stand and enter, was open to only two of the Israelites of that first generation—Caleb and Joshua. As spies in the Promised Land, they had seen the fortified cities and the armed giants with their own eyes. But they had remembered God's promise and were confident that He would deliver the land into their hands. Forty years later, Joshua and Caleb led the new generation across the River Jordan into the Promised Land!

If we fail on our first lap around, there will be another opportunity to face the same principle. We will get another choice between standing on God's Word or refusing to obey Him. Often we do not even recognize a situation as God's confrontation with a problem until we have failed it once or twice. Here is one such experience.

A woman had heard me talk about the Law of the Four Ps and the three alternatives in facing the problem. She recognized that for years she had been taking laps around a problem which had crystallized into resentment toward her mother. Upon returning home, she prayed that God would help her forgive her mother and love her. She fully expected something to happen to bring about a change in her feelings.

Something did happen—the situation took a drastic turn for the worse. She discovered that her mother had hidden some correspondence from her. The hurt was so deep that she exploded in a fit of anger, accusing her mother of trying to manipulate her life. Later that evening, she realized that God had brought her into the difficult situation to provide her with an opportunity to forgive her mother. Having failed in the problem, she knew that she could expect another lap. She decided to be on her guard for another confrontation with her mother.

A week went by and she didn't see her mother. But one evening, her husband told her that their daughter, who was away at college, had failed a class and he had permitted her to transfer to another course. While her husband was still speaking, the old familiar resentment began to rise within her: "They always do things behind my back...my husband and daughter and my mother...." Suddenly she saw the pattern of her own thoughts! This was the other lap she had been expecting. For the first time she realized that the problem wasn't resentment toward her mother; that was just a symptom. The problem was her own pride which often manifested itself in a strong tendency to be in charge of every situation and manipulate others according to her own will.

Silently she prayed, "God, forgive me. Thank You for showing me the way I really am. Take my prideful ego and as I yield myself to You, make me the mother, wife and daughter You want me to be."

Her husband looked at her with concern and continued, "Susan and I didn't want to worry you. We knew how much you wanted her to be a lawyer. But she really is much happier with the prospect of becoming a veterinarian. You know she has always loved to care for sick animals." The crisis point had passed, and the mother was able to smile and say honestly that she was happy her daughter was doing what she had always wanted to do.

A few days later when this woman went to see her mother, she discovered that the old resentment had melted away. She was able to understand that her mother had hidden those letters in order to save her from hurt. She could ask forgiveness for the angry remarks she had made the last time they were together. For the first time in many years she felt genuine love for her mother.

After many years in the wilderness—with repeated laps around the same problem—she had at last been able to recognize God's way of presenting her with the choice of trusting His principles or continuing in her own stubborn way, resulting in a final perishing in the wilderness. By standing on God's principle (that is, yielding her pride and asking forgiveness and help), she was able to enter her promised land—a warm and genuine relationship, not only with her mother but also with her husband and daughter. For years, they had suffered under her continual compulsion to control and manipulate.

God is patient and permits us another lap. This continues until we have succeeded in the problem or become so hardened that another lap will make no difference whatsoever. The laps become gradually more severe—or obvious—in order to bring a recognition of wrong reaction. God doesn't want to press us into a severe problem. He longs to show us that a difficult situation is always a doorway to the promised land—if we are willing to meet His conditions.

Once I went to the house of a potter in Peru and watched him carefully form and shape clay vessels. Then he put them in a hot oven to bake. After a certain length of time he opened the oven door and I felt the blast of the heat against my face. The potter pulled out one of the vessels, flicked the rim, and I could hear it go clunk. He returned the pot to the oven and I asked him, "How do you know when it is done?"

Smilingly, he replied, "When it sings! When I flick the rim and it gives out a beautiful resonant note, then I know it is ready."

God permits us to stay in the heat of the problem, lap after lap, until we have learned to sing. Then we are ready to move into our provision. We have become vessels prepared to be filled with the abundant love, joy and peace He has promised.

chapter six

The Religious Question

How we come through the problem—or wilderness—depends on our response to temptation. We have mentioned that temptation means putting to the proof—whether for good or evil.

In the New Testament, the word translated *trial* (or *test*) and the word translated *temptation* come from the same Greek word. Although I have thus far used the words interchangeably, as the Greeks did, I see a major difference between trial and temptation. God puts us to the proof for good purposes; trial comes from God and is *external*. In contrast, Satan puts us to the proof for evil or malicious purposes; temptation comes from Satan and is *internal*.

When we are in the midst of temptation God's principle will always be questioned. This is the essence of temptation! We shall refer to this critical point in our journey through the wilderness as the religious question.

This question may take any number of forms, but it always amounts to a doubting of God's Word or His intentions: "Hath God said...?" It always seeks to dishonor God.

In the Beginning

Temptation came to Eve in the form of the religious question. In the middle of the garden stood two trees upon which the destiny of mankind was to be determined. The simplicity seems like a "fairy tale" to some, but to the Bible student the story continues to go deeper and deeper in meaning. Life was attached to one tree. Man and woman were allowed to eat of it. It was only after tragedy that the tree of life took on new and significant meaning.

The second tree was the tree of the knowledge of good and evil. Prohibition was clear; do not eat on the threat of death. Bonhoeffer makes it clear that the tree of life is only a danger when the tree of death has had its effect.

The creation of Eve sets the stage for an encounter of the three players: God, Eve and Satan. It is evident that you cannot lay the blame for the fall on Satan alone, nor on Eve or Adam alone.

Genesis 3:1 says that the serpent came to Eve and said, "Indeed, has God said, 'You shall not eat from any tree of the garden'?" The first question was designed to test Eve to see if she remembered what God had said. What did she say? "From the fruit of the trees of the garden we may eat; but from the fruit of the tree which is in the middle of the garden God has said, 'You shall not eat from it or touch it, lest you die' " (vv. 2,3).

Satan then makes Eve feel ashamed of her naive and simplistic obedience. Her childlike trust withers under the serpent's insinuation and innuendo: "Stupid, childish girl." He throws doubt on God's love and motives by saying, "You surely shall not die! For God knows that in the day you eat from it your eyes will be opened, and you will be like God, knowing good and evil" (vv. 4,5). God's will is shown to be legalistic; He desires to hold you back from progress and self-development.

The religious question always strikes at the heart of the matter and forces us to make a decision. Shall I believe God's Word and obey Him—or shall I ignore Him and follow my own inclinations?

Satan's Access

Temptation comes to a person from the tempter or Satan. He is not an abstract principle, but a real personality, created by God, who refused to keep his first assignment. He appears on the scene of human activity without formal introduction or previous explanation as to his origin. As simplistic as it may sound, I believe in the "talking serpent."

Satan has amazingly effective access to what the theologians call the *sensorium* or the seat of sensation in the human brain. From this center, sense impressions are transmitted to the rest of the body by means of the nerves. It is clear biblically that Satan can implant desire or despair into the senses and the imagination until the sensorium is inflamed beyond one's ability or willingness to manage its demands.

The more a person gauges truth by his or her senses and sense-knowledge, the more power temptation will have in his or her life (see Eph. 4:19). The reasoning seems to go like this: If I have a sexual urge, a hunger or an intense desire, it must be God-given. Consequently, the natural thing to do is to satisfy it accordingly.

God's principles are no longer the measuring stick. What I feel becomes more important than what God has said.

God always arranges circumstances in such a way that the religious question will face us, because until it *has* been faced, there is always the possibility of double-mindedness, self-will, ego or weakness hiding in our hearts—ready to trip us up at a critical moment.

But James says clearly that we must not *blame* our temptations on God.

Let no one say when he is tempted, "I am being tempted by God"; for God cannot be tempted by evil, and He Himself does not tempt any one. But each one is tempted when he is carried away and enticed by his own lust. Then when lust has conceived, it gives birth to sin; and when sin is accomplished, it brings forth death (James 1:13-15).

There's nothing new about trying to blame God for our temptation. In the Garden of Eden, both Eve and then Adam blamed God for their predicament. God, who is untemptable, never tempts anyone to wrong action or with a hostile purpose.

Temptation, says James, comes from within. When something called lust is inflamed and enticed, it can "carry us away"—to make and act on decisions that we would not make if we were acting entirely on our own will.

The person who gives way to internal temptation while in the midst of external trial must see the difference between the two and never blame the "damage" on God. Some time ago our area was struck by a fierce hurricane. Most people talked about the terrible damage caused by the hurricane, but that wasn't actually the case. In that hurricane were thirty tornados, and that is what caused the destruction. To make the analogy clear, in our spiritual lives, the "tornados" are always the work of Satan who sets out to destroy and who works in the midst of the "hurricane" or the trial sent by God.

The tempter, in the midst of the events of life, seeks to inflame illegal desire and draw us away from God and His love. God, on the other hand, allows or initiates the external events in order to confirm our faith and establish His righteousness. Temptation, as separate from trial or testing, begins when the internal events start to develop.

James uses another image to show how Satan works. He says that something is conceived in a person's sensorium. Just as a sperm enters a woman's womb, unites with the ovum and grows into a child, satanic suggestion ("Has God said?") enters the sensorium, which is "ripe" because of one's fallen nature. Just as the endometrium receives the fertilized egg and feeds and nourishes it, so lust, greed or innate and undisciplined desire to have something or be someone great nourishes a "fetus" which, when born, is, paradoxically, death.

An Easy Way Out?

The religious question must be faced and answered by all of us—and in all major areas of our lives. In effect, God says in His Word: "If you do these things that I command you, you will live and eat the good of the land...don't steal, don't lie, don't commit adultery, don't covet, don't have other gods before me, don't kill, honor your parents...." Then He sums it up with these words, "Love the Lord with all your heart and mind and might and love your neighbor as yourself" (see Matt. 22:37).

Did God really say that? All of us have been faced

with this question, as well as the suggestion, ''Those rules were made by a mean old God who doesn't want us to enjoy life.'' Almost every young couple in love faces the religious question, ''Did God really say we shouldn't have sexual intercourse before we're married? But we really love each other and we're going to get married someday. What harm can it possibly do?''

The religious question will always suggest that your own way is the easier and better way (while God's way is difficult and could not possibly lead to the fulfillment of your dreams and ambitions). While you are in the midst of trial, the religious question will present itself in the form of deception, rationalization and excuses—and you will find that your reason and your senses are most likely to be in direct opposition to God's Word.

I once counseled a single woman who was torn with desire for a man who was already married. His marriage wasn't a happy one and from their first meeting they struck up a friendship based on common interests—including a common faith in God. Both were what I would call sincere Christians who wanted to obey God's will. Their story followed a classic pattern. They soon discovered that their friendship had grown into ''spiritual love.'' Later their affections grew stronger and they found themselves on the verge of open adultery. At this point the woman came to me for advice.

''Couldn't it be possible that God led us together?'' she asked hopefully. ''Couldn't it be God's will? Our relationship is so beautiful—it seems so right—and we feel so close to God when we're together.''

''What has God said about adultery?'' I countered.

''We know that,'' she admitted, ''but this is different. We would get married if only his wife would give him a divorce.''

"What are you going to do about God's commandment?'' I repeated.

She looked down and murmured, ''I don't feel we are doing anything wrong. How can God be opposed to something so beautiful?''

My next question was, ''If you don't think God is serious about adultery, how do you know what He is serious about? Are you going to judge by your feelings or by what God has said?''

There were tears in her eyes as she acknowledged, ''I understand what you mean. I'll have to go home and pray about it some more.''

Three days later she was back, looking drawn and pale. ''You know,'' she began, ''I've so wanted this thing to be real; I've never wanted anything more in my life. But when I went home from your office, I read God's commandments and saw that what we were doing was against His Word. God calls it *sin*. It was an awful label to put on something I felt was the most wonderful thing that had happened to me.'' She bit her lip and was silent for a moment. ''For several agonizing hours I wasn't so sure I wanted to turn away from it even though I knew it was wrong. I was afraid I'd never know real happiness away from him—and I was almost willing to turn my back on God for that. Never had temptation looked sweeter. Then I decided that deep down in my heart I wanted God's will more than anything else—even if it meant I would never know the love of a man.''

For two days and nights following her decision, she said, she battled with constant waves of longing. ''There were times when I walked the floor and said over and over again, 'Jesus, Jesus, I love You, Jesus.' I couldn't even read my Bible because my thoughts would stray.''

Our interviews concluded with this statement: ''On the third day, the battle lessened in severity. It still hurts, but I feel as if I've come out of prison. I can breathe again and I have a solid feeling inside that God's Word is more real than anything else in this world. I feel safer now than I have ever felt before. I know God will do what He has said.''

Less than a year later, the woman was married to another Christian. She told me, ''God's promised land is ever so much better than the things you give up to follow His command.'' Temptation will always suggest an alternate route to the promised land. But the alternate road dead-ends in the wilderness.

What Has God Said?

The religious question will also suggest a clever twisting of God's instructions. Therefore, it is essential that we understand clearly what God says in the first place. It should be elementary for Christians to familiarize themselves with God's Word. It is our guidebook on our journey through the wilderness to the promised land. If we follow the Law of the Four Ps, we need the Bible to check us at every point along the way.

First, check the promise. Is it according to God's Word? Don't take a promise out of context or accept a personal promise which you assume is from God without checking it against the character and principles of the Bible. You may have a strong desire for something and ask God for it with intensity. In prayer, or through circumstances, you may feel that God is telling you that He will grant your prayer. Always check your desire against what the Bible has to say. If it is inconsistent with either God's character or Word, then the promise is a false one.

A woman once prayed for the Lord to give her a beautiful antique dresser that had been standing in a neighbor's garage—thinking the neighbor did not really want it. After much petitioning, the woman thought God impressed on her that He would give her the dresser. After weeks of waiting, she thought God wanted her to go and claim it from the neighbor. As you can imagine, the result was a very unpleasant episode! The dresser was a family heirloom and the owner had planned to refinish it. Argument, hard feelings and disappointment followed.

If the woman who prayed for the dresser had understood God's principles, she would have recognized that He commands us not to covet what belongs to anyone else. She had coveted and let herself be led astray by her own strong desires—prompted by the tempter who had suggested that God had said something in direct contradiction to His own commandments.

Beware of standing on the wrong promises. God will not promise you anything in contradiction to His own Word. Don't covet your neighbor's new car, his house, his dog or his wife! And don't ever let yourself be deceived into believing that God promises to give you anything that rightfully belongs to someone else. Those are the kinds of suggestions the religious question will put to us.

If your debts amount to $697.66, and you pray for God to provide what you need to pay them off, you may discover a billfold on the bus seat beside you. Inside it is exactly $700! Next comes the religious question like a flood.

IN THE FACE OF TEMPTATION

"Did God really say you shouldn't steal?"

"Yes, that's one of the Ten Commandments, and it's in the New Testament, too."

"But don't you realize that God provided that billfold for you? It's exactly the amount you're praying for. Nobody will ever know you took it, just slip the money out and leave the billfold in the seat."

God never contradicts Himself or goes against His own Word. Study the Bible, learn its principles and be ready to face the religious question in all of its persuasive power.

Remember the questions we said were apt to come following your salvation? "Are you sure you are saved?"

"I think I am."

"But you don't feel saved and you don't act saved."

"But I believe in Jesus Christ and God's Word says I am saved."

Stand on God's Word against your feelings, emotions and rationalizations.

A mother receives the promise that God will save her son. She goes home rejoicing—and the next time she sees him he is high on dope. Now comes the religious question.

"Did God really say He was going to save your son?"

"Yes, I'm sure."

"But look at him now. Do you think God can save him? Look at his miserable condition. God will never be able to reach him!"

Can you stand on God's Word, keep your eyes on Him instead of what your senses or reason tell you? God has saved dope addicts before. He'll do it again.

God says, "I will save your husband and make your home into a haven of Christian love and unity." There is your promise. Now comes the condition—the principle: "If you will trust Me and do your part as a Christian, submitting to your husband just as he is."

"But, Lord...."

That evening your husband gets drunk, curses your "silly religion" and leaves the house in anger. Up comes the religious question.

"Did God really say He was going to save your husband?"

"Yes."

"He'll never be able to change him!"

Can you stand on the promise, or do you give in to the temptation?

"God can't do it. My husband is just too stubborn." That reaction will earn you another lap through the problem!

When God says He'll take you to a promised land, you can only get there if you follow His instructions. The religious question will always suggest alternate methods.

Abraham's Story

We are now going to take the story of God's dealings with Abraham in regard to fulfilling His promise that even though Abraham was an old man, he would have a son and that his descendants would be like the stars—too many to count! This is recorded in Genesis chapters 15 through 21.

Abram believed God's promise and went home and told his wife, Sarai. Since they both were old, they were certain they could have no children and reasoned that if God's promise was to become a reality, Abram would have to father a child by Sarai's servant.

But God had not instructed Abram concerning Hagar.

Abram and Sarai followed their own logic and reasoning, prompted by the religious question: "If God said you were to have many children, you better find a young woman who can bear them."

Since they did not follow God's instructions by waiting for God to give them a son, they found themselves on another lap through a problem made more severe by their wrong decision. Hagar, the servant girl, became pregnant and bore a son, Ishmael. But ill feeling had entered the household between Sarai and Hagar—and later Ishmael's descendants caused troubles for Israel.

Thirteen years after Ishmael's birth, God came to Abram again and told him He would make an everlasting covenant with him and his descendants. God said Abram would be the father of many nations and changed his name to Abraham—father of many nations. God also said that Sarai's name would be Sarah (Princess) and that she would bear a son.

Abraham threw himself down on the ground to worship the Lord, but he laughed to himself because he was 100 years old and Sarah was 90. How could they possibly have a child? Abraham thought he must have heard wrong, and so he said to God, "Yes, do bless Ishmael" (17:18, TLB).

"No," God replied. God was very specific and this time Abraham didn't try any short cuts of his own. He believed God, and after a year Sarah bore him a son and they named him Isaac. God intended to put Abraham to the test before He could fulfill His promise to make Isaac the father of many nations.

Later on God again tested Abraham's faith and obedience. Listen to God's instructions: "Take now your son, your only son, whom you love, Isaac, and go to the land of Moriah; and offer him there as a burnt offering on one of the mountains of which I will tell you'' (22:2).

The next morning Abraham got up early, chopped wood for a fire upon the altar, saddled his donkey and took with him his son, Isaac. Now you can imagine the barrage of religious questions swirling through this father's mind? ''Did God really say to sacrifice Isaac? What about the covenant He made with Isaac? He promised to make him the father of many nations and said His covenant would be with him forever and with his descendants. If God is going to keep His covenant with Isaac, you better not sacrifice him.''

''I must obey God's Word.''

''You're being a fool, Abraham. You're going to destroy your covenant with God. If Isaac is killed there is no one left for God to use. God doesn't really mean for you to do it; it doesn't make sense. Besides, Isaac is everything you have in life—your only son—what do you think his mother will say?''

These questions cut to the core of Abraham's heart. This was the area where he was the most vulnerable. Isaac, his only son, meant more to him than anything else on earth. God had to bring Abraham to the test to see if Isaac meant more to him than obedience to God Himself. If there was any doublemindedness in Abraham, it would show itself now. And if there was any doublemindedness, God could not permit Abraham to receive the fulfillment of His great promise.

But Abraham stood firm and moved ahead to prepare for the sacrifice. Just as he lifted the knife, the angel of God called to him saying, ''Do not stretch out your hand against the lad, and do nothing to him; for now I know that you fear God, since you have not withheld your son, your only son, from Me'' (22:12). Then Abraham noticed a ram caught by its horns in a bush. He sacrificed it instead of his son and named the place ''Jehovah provides''—and it still goes by that name to this day. Abraham proved God could provide! He faced Satan's religious questions, choosing to obey God's Word.

Do you see how these dealings with Abraham followed the Law of the Four Ps? He received the promise, followed by the principle, ''Obey Me and trust Me.'' Then came the problem, and it looked as if the entire promise was being taken away. But Abraham stood on the principle and came through into the fulfillment of his provision.

Obedience alone will take you through to God's provision. But the religious question will have to be faced and answered. Be sure of what God wants you to do. Understand the principle, and be prepared to hold onto it, no matter how convincing the religious question may be!

chapter seven

The Examinations

There's an old story about a man walking down the street and seeing the devil on the curbstone crying bitterly. "What's the matter?" questioned the bystander.

The devil answered, "I'm always getting blamed for things I didn't get a chance to do!" The devil has long been our favorite scapegoat. When we do something we shouldn't, we say, "I didn't mean to, but the devil tempted me."

In reality, temptation hangs in a delicate balance between three participants: God, ourselves and the devil.

Yes, the devil is very much involved. He is a power to be reckoned with. But powerful as Satan may be, he is *not* the prime mover in temptation. God is. He ordained the workings of the Law of the Four Ps. Let's go over it again. He gave the promise and the principle and placed the problem as a preparation for receiving the provision. Central to the problem is temptation with the religious questions bombarding us. This presents us with the choice of obeying or disobeying God's Word. God puts us to the test only in order to prepare us to receive the good things He has promised us.

How, in practical experience, does God test a person? For an answer, we take 2 Chronicles 32:31: "God left him [Hezekiah] alone only to test him, that He might know all that was in his heart."

This may raise another question. The Bible says God left Hezekiah. How can this be consistent with the many passages stating that God will never leave us or forsake us? Psalm 139 tells us: "If I ascend to heaven, Thou art there; if I make my bed in Sheol, behold, Thou art there. If I take the wings of the dawn, if I dwell in the remotest part of the sea, even there thy hand will lead me" (vv. 8-10).

Yet we are told that God left Hezekiah to test him and see what he was really like. We must come to see the difference between God's omnipresence and our conscious presence of Him. God left Hezekiah only in the sense that He removed Hezekiah's awareness of His presence. God was still there, but Hezekiah couldn't feel Him. It is when Daddy is gone that the real test of obedience comes to the children.

"Now, kids, when I'm gone, don't fight, and remember which TV programs are forbidden."

"Sure, Dad, we'll be good!"

Four hours later Daddy comes home to find the house is filled with guilt and conviction!

How else can God find out what is in us? If we feel Him there all the time and we have that wonderful assurance of His presence, we won't be tempted to distrust Him in the problem.

The Silent Teacher

It has taken me a long time to see that, as a master teacher, God very carefully gives the promise, speaks in no uncertain terms as to what the principles are, and *then refuses to talk once the exam begins*. Anyone who has been through higher education knows that the teacher does not talk during the exam. Lessons are given, lectures are over, then it is exam time. The teacher sits by quietly or leaves the room. No questions are answered now, unless it is one of procedure or clarification.

How does this work in spiritual application? God gives the promise and the principle. He makes them clear and then withdraws the consciousness of His presence. He does not, I repeat, does not, withdraw His presence, but He withdraws our consciousness of His presence. Then the test or the exam begins. In the absence of the joyful and powerful sense of the presence of my Lord, the tempter appears. Now the test has become a temptation. I call out to the Lord. Most often the heavens are brass and the earth is silent.

In the absence of His manifest presence and in His silence, I am about to find out what is actually in my heart. The only appropriate answer is that cold, hard, objective truth, "It is written." Standing on what God said during the exam forms in you a trust, an endurance, the kind of Christian character that is unattainable apart from the test.

If Eve had felt God's presence in the garden, there wouldn't have been any problem. She would have walked up to the tree and God would have said, "Now, Eve, remember: That's the tree I told you not to eat from. Be careful. That beautiful creature with the smooth voice is the devil trying to make you disobey Me and get you into trouble.''

No, it doesn't work that way. God's purpose in withdrawing our consciousness of His presence is to make us face temptation and the religious question on the basis of His principle alone!

If the Israelites had felt the power of God's presence when Moses left them to go up on Mount Sinai, they would never have been faced with the temptation to make an image of a golden calf. God would have been there, assuring them: ''Here I am, My children. Don't worry, I'll always be with you. You will always be able to *feel* Me near you.''

If God is to reveal to us what is really in our hearts, He must withdraw from us the sense-experience of His presence. Satan is then permitted to go to work with the religious question—and we are in the middle. The balance depends on us. We are forced to choose between Satan's suggestions and God's instructions.

When God gets ready to work with us in a certain area, He withdraws our consciousness of His presence. Then Satan comes in and says, ''God is gone now.''

Feeling lonely and depressed, we agree, ''Yes, He is gone now.''

Satan reminds us, ''Remember how you felt a few weeks ago? His presence made you feel warm and excited and challenged?''

''Yes, that's right,'' we respond miserably.

The tempter continues, ''God has forsaken you. What you need is a good stiff drink to cheer you up!''

''But God doesn't want me to drink.''

The religious questions continue: ''Doesn't He? He

knows how weak you are and that you *need* a drink. He won't care if you have just one. It will make you feel a lot better. Go ahead...."

So we succumb to the temptation to go to the bar—and have just one and then another and another. The next morning we feel even more miserable and mad at the devil. "He made me do it!"

Oh, no, he didn't! He only brought out what was already in our hearts. If no leanings in that direction had been inside, Satan could have had no appeal in that area. We need to understand this principle.

Let's look at another weakness. God says, "Christian, don't commit adultery."

"Yes, Lord. I understand that." Then God withdraws the consciousness of His presence and the temptation presents itself.

"Christian, you know your wife doesn't really understand you."

"That's right. She wasn't very nice at breakfast this morning."

Now that the door is open, Satan continues. "She doesn't really care about how hard you work or what a wonderful Christian you are. Why don't you have a nice long talk with that pretty secretary of yours? She understands what a good job you are doing and what you go through."

God desires to give every Christian a solid marriage, and He wants to use us to help others who have problems with sex and marriage. What do you think God has to bring each of us through in order to prepare us for this provision?

Spiritual leaders aren't immune to temptation. In fact, they are prime targets because God wants to bring us over into the promised land so that we can show others the way through the problem. And there are no short cuts between promise/principle/problem/provision for people who are "God's special servants." They must go through the problem to get into the provision—and in the problem they are faced with the temptation and the religious question. If there is something inside that needs to surface, it will show itself.

When I first understood that God was calling me to the ministry, I went through a wonderful period of joy in His presence. I thought, *This is wonderful. I am going to serve God and He will be right next to me for the rest of my life.* Then I lost the *feeling* of God's presence and plunged into a time of conflict, fears and doubts.

The religious question pounded me, "Do you mean God called *you* to the ministry? That's ridiculous! You know you don't have what it takes. You're even afraid of facing people. God will never be able to use *you.*" For months the conflict went on. From a rational point of view, the religious questions all made sense. I wasn't the studious type. I had been a rough-mouthed sailor when God touched me. How could I ever tell anybody about God and His kingdom?

In Jeremiah 1:4-8, I found recorded a conversation between God and Jeremiah which meant much to me:

Now the word of the Lord came to me saying, "Before I formed you in the womb I knew you, and before you were born I consecrated you; I have appointed you a prophet to the nations." Then I said, "Alas, Lord God! Behold, I do not know how to speak, because I am a youth." But the Lord said to me, "Do not say, 'I am a youth,' because everywhere I send you, you shall go, and all that I command you, you shall speak. Do not be afraid of them, for I am with you to deliver you," declares the Lord.

But the religious question came back at me, "That was for Jeremiah! Why don't you forget the crazy idea and do something sensible for a living." The battle went on until one day I walked into the pulpit where I was to preach as a student minister, stood there facing the congregation half-scared and said very firmly under my breath, "God has called me to preach. I know I'm not good enough, but He's going to make me able and I won't turn back!" Immediately the conflicting thoughts calmed down. I opened my mouth and began to speak—without any sensation of God's presence but with a new determination that God's Word was all I needed to stand on.

Most of us use our feelings to measure our so-called spirituality. We say, "I feel spiritual today. I can just *feel* God's presence. It gives me goosebumps! Wasn't that a wonderful meeting last night? Couldn't you *feel* the Holy Spirit?" Then when the sensations and feelings are absent, we get down in the dumps and are prone to respond with, "I feel so depressed. I must not be very spiritual today. Perhaps I had better pray more—or go to another meeting tonight. God will be there."

We tend to be like the young man who went through the wedding ceremony and later, on the sidewalk outside the church, he turned to his bride and said, "Honey, I don't feel married, do you?"

She quickly replied, "Dear, you'd better adjust your feelings to fit the facts! Believe me, you are *now* married!"

While we are in the problem we will not be able to

sense God's presence. God wants to free us from a dependency on our feelings in order that we can learn to stand on His Word alone. The following might be an actual explanation from God as to His workings:

I'll be with you here in the wilderness. I give you My promise and I will explain My working principle. I will make sure that you understand. But when you get into the problem, I must remove your awareness of My presence. I'll be with you, but you will not be aware of it. It will seem as if you are all alone, facing the temptation and the religious question. It is necessary that I do this that you might see what I see in your heart. I promise you that over in the promised land you will feel My presence again.

When God allows us to sense His presence, it is on either side of the problem. In fact, the absence of a sensation of God's presence is one of the characteristics of the time in the problem. If we panic in the problem, as the Israelites did—time after time—and cry out for God to come and help us, He will; but the result will be another lap around the mountain and an extended stay in the wilderness.

A friend of mine had an amazing experience while he was in Bible college. One night he was alone in his room praying when the presence of God filled the room in a remarkable way. My friend was both excited and grateful. He could sense God saying, "I will never leave you or forsake you." It was a wonderful promise.

Then God withdrew the manifestation of His presence—for two whole years. Never once during that time did my friend feel the least awareness of God's presence. But he repeated to himself, and to us: "God has told me He will never leave me or forsake me. I don't feel Him, but I know His promise. He is with me because He said so." After two years God's presence came again—more real than ever before. He felt called as a missionary to the Amazon Indians and is now deep in the jungles of Peru—alone. But he has learned to walk on the naked word of God.

The desire to know good from evil got the better of Eve. God wants us to be where we trust His judgment and take His word for what is good and evil. We don't need to be familiar with evil in order to choose good. Familiarity with evil is dangerous, even when it goes by the label of enlightened understanding. Paul tells us, "Don't even think about such things" (see Eph. 5:12). Until we decide to put away our curiosity and obey God wholeheartedly, we will remain in the wilderness and be constantly prodded by the religious question. Temptation will hang in the balance until we make a definite decision and stand for or against God's Word.

The Razor's Edge

Temptation isn't real unless it involves the actual possibility of failure—a moment where you face the issue squarely and it is almost a toss-up which way you will take. Temptation looks so sweet—so sensible—so logical—you are on the verge of trading what it offers for what God has said. When you have faced that kind of decision, you have moved from lip service to God to wholehearted willingness to obey Him regardless of what it may cost you.

Dashing into the bathroom, a woman slammed the door, screaming, "I'll cut my wrists!"

Confused and distraught her husband said, "All right, I'll stay home. I won't go to the meeting." According to this young husband, that was one of the great mistakes of his life. From that exact moment, his difficult marriage became worse. Once he had buckled, she controlled the marriage. From that day on they both became increasingly worldly, and the young husband suffered in a wilderness for a long and lonely period.

That particular meeting had been called so his church could help him be a better husband, prepare him for fatherhood and give direction for the call of God that was evident on his life. Standing at the bathroom door, this man didn't realize that it was not actually his wife who was screaming. He wasn't prepared to "stand firm against the schemes of the devil" (Eph. 6:11). No, I do not believe that all hysteria or marital discord is "of the devil." But I do know this couple, and their story records an extremely clear case of what I call "the razor's edge."

Standing there, a young, confused husband wanted to do what is right. But he faced a blast of accusation and attack that seemed more than he could bear, forcing, ever forcing an ultimate decision: do you do what is biblically correct and trust God for the results, or do you yield? By his own admission to me later, he really did know what he should have done.

The razor's edge is that precise psychological moment when, under test (external) and temptation (internal), we are forced to make that decision for which we are accountable before God and humanity.

On Mt. Moriah, at the crucial moment of Abraham's temptation/test, the angel of the Lord said, "Do not stretch out your hand against the lad, and do nothing to him, for now I know that you fear God, since you have not withheld your son, your only son, from Me'' (Gen. 22:17).

God, it seems, pressed into Abraham, again and again until He touched Abraham's razor's edge. After that was clear, the pressure let off, and he got on with his journey. How does God press into one until He finds the razor's edge? Hebrews, a book that carefully keeps the threats and promises of God together, offers us a route that is quite clear, ''For the word of God is living and active and sharper than any two-edged sword, and piercing as far as the division of soul and [the immortal] spirit, of both joints and marrow, and able to judge the thoughts and intentions of the heart. All things are open and laid bare to the eyes of Him with whom we have to do'' (4:12,13). In teaching on body, soul and spirit, some make such clear categories that they seem to say that you can know in a very distinctive manner when a thing is ''soulish'' or rooted in the human spirit. They would use a diagram something like this:

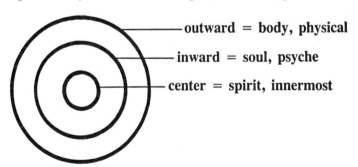

The human spirit is a kind of holy of holies (and so the teaching goes) and is what worships God. Mary, in the Magnificat, seemed to make this distinction when she said, ''My soul exalts the Lord, and my spirit has rejoiced in God my Savior'' (Luke 1:46,47).

For our use, however, I should like to offer a different kind of diagram which may shed some light on how temptation works.

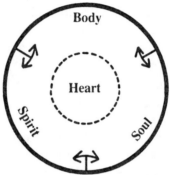

On the outward edges of a personality there does seem to be a difference between what is soulish and what is spiritual (see 1 Thess. 5:23). (We do know that the senses [or the sensorium] dwell in the soul, and the "image of God" basically dwells in the human spirit.) But generally we are whole persons, not so easily "divided." In fact, we can be divided only by the living and two-edged sword of God's Word. That which happens in one category of our beings, whether soul, spirit or body, immediately and unavoidably affects all of the other parts, for we are whole persons.

So the *heart* (a tremendous word study in Scripture, especially in the original language), designated by the dotted lines in the center of the diagram, signifies the whole person, in all of his or her "parts." Moses says God is after what is in our hearts!

Hebrews 4:12 states that the living and powerful Word is acting in us for salvation or judgment, but never without results. The writer of Hebrews then says the Word penetrates a person's innermost being, all the way to the heart, the very center of personality. The Word bounces around internally, distinguishing, judging, deciding and discerning, searching for the things hidden in darkness and the disclosure of motives.

As the Word searches us, forces us to stand in God's presence (head lifted, neck stretched, so we can't hide like Adam and Eve), it is not to condemn, but to redeem. Jesus' intent is to set us free. It is a process as well as a happening.

What is manifested in temptation is never a surprise to God, but it surely is to us. Often, I have been as surprised at the strength of my obedience as I was surprised at what was revealed as I entered temptation.

I wonder if that was the case with Joseph the son of Jacob. To this young man came the *promise*: the sheaves will bow down. Little did he know how much of the *principle* of God's law and God's covenant was written on his heart. Suddenly, he was plunged into the *problem*, and the season of testing and temptation was upon him. He was placed in the pit and sold into Egypt and proceeded through some twelve or thirteen years of exam. Upon being released he was tempted by Potiphar's wife in an unbelievable way. He held to God's principles in the absence of the manifest presence of the God of the covenant without wavering. He endured a kind of loneliness that only a Hebrew can experience in their kind of covenantal family bonds.

When the exam was over, God began the *provision*, giving interpretation to the dreams and exalting Joseph to the throne of Egypt. Joseph could not have been raised to such honor (provision) until he had passed through a deep abasement to come to the razor's edge, as the psalmist says, "The word of the Lord tested"

Joseph (105:19).

Being Prepared

One illustrative incident that stands out in my memory happened when I was a very young minister teaching in Bible college. A man came to me with a tempting proposition. He said, "I need some money to buy five used cars to resell. I'll give you one of the cars free and clear if you will sign my note." Immediately I felt impressed that God didn't want me to sign that note. He would provide a car for me some other way.

God withdrew my consciousness of His presence and my old car began to look even older—the thought of a new car looked better all the time. I went home to my wife and said, "Judy, we ought to sign this." Her reply was, "The Lord tells me we shouldn't."

The religious questions came: "Who is head of this house? Who makes the decisions?" She succumbed. We signed the note. I didn't get the car I had been promised, and we were transferred to another Bible college.

Some months later I returned on a visit and walked into the local bank to greet my friend there. I was shocked to have him say to me, "Bob, I've been looking for you...." Yes. The car salesman had defaulted on his payments. My name was on the papers, and I had to assume financial responsibility for the debt. My reputation and my Christian witness were marred. But God had taught me a lesson!

In my heart had been the desire to get something for nothing. Many of us are vulnerable here. In God's purpose He could have provided me with a new car. But first He wanted to expose that little something lurking inside me. God wanted to bring it out into the open so that I could have an opportunity to turn it over to Him.

Before I could come into my provision, God had to expose me to temptation. In this case, I failed the test because my own desire for a new car was stronger than my willingness to obey God's instructions. The result was another lap around the mountain—and an extended stay in the wilderness!

Is it becoming increasingly clear to you that before we can move into our promised land we must be prepared?

Take the time to read Psalm 119 in a different translation from the one you ordinarily use. I suggest the New International Version or the New American Standard Bible. The commentators say this was a psalm written by a young man who was being persecuted for his confidence in Jehovah while attempts were being made from all sides and from all sources to move him away from God's Word! The German version has the appropriate introduction, ''The Christian's golden ABCs of the praise, love, power and use of the Word of God.''

When I use the word *principle*, I am referring to the living Word of God, Old Testament and New—His sayings, testimonies, ways, judgments, precepts, commandments, laws, statutes and truth. In the New Testament, of course, this has been personified in the Word becoming flesh in the person of our Lord Jesus Christ (see Matt. 5:17; Rom. 8:3).

chapter eight

Christ in the Wilderness

In a very real sense, there are only two temptations in the whole Bible. All others take off from those two: Adam's and Christ's. Adam failed, and all humanity fell—and died. Christ succeeded. His victory led to Satan's fall and provides life to all who believe.

The Bible tells us that Jesus Christ was tempted in every respect as we are and it is unrealistic to think that His temptation differed from ours.

Jesus Christ was given the promise and taught the principle, then God withdrew from His Son the consciousness of His presence, and Jesus was exposed to all the forces of hell. All the religious questions Satan is capable of suggesting were thrown at our Lord and Savior. The temptation of Jesus would not have been real had it not contained the possibility of failure. Anything less would have been contrary to the principles of God. The Israelites were chosen of God to enter the

Promised Land, yet they failed to come into their full provision. Jesus Christ, God's only Son, could, conceivably, have failed as well. Although Jesus was God, He was also human, and as such He was temptable.

A Trip to the Wilderness

The Gospels tell of Jesus' temptation in the wilderness, and it is interesting to note the chronological order of events. The temptation occurred immediately after Jesus had been baptized in the Jordan River and filled with the Holy Spirit and before He entered His ministry as Messiah. Failure in the problem wouldn't have changed the fact that He was God's Son who had been filled with the Holy Spirit, but it would have adversely affected His role as Messiah, His provision.

Many Christians say, "Oh, if I could only be full of the Holy Spirit, then I wouldn't have any more problems." Take another look at the life of Jesus! God wants every one of us to be emptied of self and filled with His Holy Spirit. But when you pray to be filled with the Holy Spirit, don't expect all your problems to melt away; instead expect *new* problems. This is a necessary part of the package. The infilling of the Holy Spirit is the potential, or the promise. It must be put to the test before we can come safely into our provision.

The same principle holds true when a spaceship is built. Before it can be launched, it is tested under full power to see if all systems are go. If any defects show up during the test, the part is repaired or exchanged. When God fills us with His Holy Spirit, we are put through the test to see if our systems are go. Then we are ready to be launched on the mission He has for us.

Matthew tells us that Jesus came to the Jordan River where John was preaching and baptizing. Jesus asked to be baptized, but John didn't think this was proper. He said, "I have need to be baptized by you" (Matt. 3:14). But Jesus insisted.

Commentators suggest that in presenting Himself for baptism, Jesus fulfilled righteousness. When He later allowed Himself to be driven into the wilderness to be tempted, it was so that His righteousness could be tried.

Jesus knew that He had come to fulfill God's law and the writings of the prophets. He was thoroughly familiar with every word of God written in the Scriptures. These were the principles on which He stood.

There are only a few glimpses of Jesus' childhood and youth in the Scriptures, but they are sufficient to establish that He was exceptionally well acquainted with the Scriptures. (See Luke 2:40-50.)

Jesus was baptized by John and:

...while He was praying, heaven was opened, and the Holy Spirit descended upon Him in bodily form like a dove, and a voice came out of heaven, "Thou art My beloved Son, in Thee I am well-pleased" (Luke 3:21,22).

There is general agreement among theologians that this double baptism of water and the Holy Spirit constituted the preparation for Jesus' messianic ministry. But the preparation wasn't complete. Instead of setting out immediately on His life-giving mission, we find that "immediately the Spirit impelled Him to go out into the wilderness. And He was in the wilderness forty days being tempted by Satan" (Mark 1:12,13).

A Christian who experiences an infilling or a baptism of the Holy Spirit may be told by well-meaning but misled fellow-believers that he or she is now ready and prepared for "doing a great work for God." He or she may be totally unprepared for what comes next—a trip to the wilderness and a confrontation with the enemy. In the problems and confusion following, many Christians have despaired and concluded that the whole experience with the Holy Spirit was a product of their own imaginations and the beginning of all their troubles.

Jesus was in the wilderness, alone with Satan, for forty days and nights without eating; and the Bible says He was hungry. The Scriptures do not state specifically that God withdrew the consciousness of His presence from Jesus, but I think we can be absolutely certain that He did. Had Jesus been able to sense God's presence, the temptation would have been a farce. We know that it was deadly serious business where His messianic role and the salvation of mankind was at stake. Luke 4 records the conflict.

Stones to Bread

Satan's first attack came in the realm of physical provision. It was a temptation in *sensuous* form, appealing to appetite, lust or greed. It had to do with Jesus' very real hunger pains—His feelings of fatigue and discomfort.

Into the sensorium (Satan clearly had access to Jesus' sensorium) came the religious question: "If you are the Son of God, tell this stone to become bread" (v.3). In effect, Satan was saying, "You may or may not be the Son of God—I cannot tell. Convince me by turning the stone into bread. You satisfy Your hunger and I will know for sure."

Jesus *knew* He was the Son of God and perfectly capable of turning that stone into bread. He was also extremely hungry. The miracle could easily be justified. But more than hunger was at stake here. Satan was suggesting that Jesus use His power to satisfy His own need; and he was also implying that His greatest need was for bread.

There is a fine line between selfishness and a legitimate love of self which Jesus told us to have (Mark 12:31): "You shall love your neighbor as yourself." Jesus had the authority to ask for blessings for others as well as for Himself, but He had come to offer Himself as the Bread of Life to those who hungered for more than physical satisfaction.

The temptation comes to every believer to use his or her authority to ask for blessings from a selfish motive. Satan suggests that this is justifiable and reasonable. ("You need a bigger house, a better job, more money. God will be glorified when you prosper; so go ahead and ask for those stones to be turned into bread!")

Jesus answered Satan, "It is written [cold, hard, objective truth], 'Man shall not live on bread alone, but on every word that proceeds out of the mouth of God' " (Matt. 4:4). The Living Bible paraphrases this saying, " 'Other things in life are much more important than bread!' " Put another way, Jesus might have said, "Obeying God takes precedence over my senses. I wait for My Father in dependence upon His bread."

Jesus chose to remain hungry but obedient to God's Word, rather than to satisfy His own physical need by provoking God. He quoted from the Scripture account of the Israelites in the wilderness; they had been tested in the same way and had failed. Listen as Moses reminded the people of God's goodness and desires for them:

> And you shall remember all the way which the
> Lord your God has led you in the wilderness these

forty years, that He might humble you, testing you, to know what was in your heart, whether you would keep His commandments or not. And He humbled you and let you be hungry, and fed you with manna which you did not know, that He might make you understand that man does not live by bread alone, but man lives by everything that proceeds out of the mouth of the Lord (Deut. 8:2,3).

The Israelites gave in to temptation and begged for bread. As a consequence they were unable to enter their Promised Land. Jesus in the wilderness won the victory—and the provision!

Worship Me

In the second temptation Satan tried to get to Jesus through His *reason*, suggesting that He doubt the ultimate truth. Who will be worshipped and obeyed?

And he led Him up and showed Him all the kingdoms of the world in a moment of time. And the devil said to Him, ''I will give You all this domain and its glory; for it has been handed over to me, and I give it to whomever I wish. Therefore if You worship before me, it shall all be yours'' (Luke 4:5-7).

Who and what we worship are the final test of our hearts. Satan knew Jesus' identity and His appointed role as Messiah and ultimate ruler of the earth. But he also knew that Jesus had been asked to go the way of the cross, the way of suffering, rejection and death. Now he offered Him a compromise—an easy way out!

I am convinced that this was no easy temptation for Jesus to face. He was alone in the wilderness, tired and hungry and not conscious of the presence of God. Had He been, the temptation to worship anyone else would have been completely meaningless. At this point, Satan appeared before Him in all his power, beauty and light. In 2 Corinthians 11:14, he is described as "an angel of light," and his appearance can be both beautiful and appealing.

A man I know had reached a crisis point in his Christian commitment and went away to fast and pray. After three days alone in a hotel room, he sensed the presence of God with him in a glorious way. The man was kneeling in prayer when it happened, and he became so overwhelmed with awe that he put his face down in the rug. There he stayed; and after a while the sense of God's presence lifted from him.

He remained with his face down and eyes tightly closed. Suddenly he "saw" a man standing before him. He was the most beautiful person he had ever seen and was surrounded by an aura of light. A strong desire to worship the beautiful apparition swept over him, and he could hear a voice, strong and smooth, saying, "If you worship me, I will give you a powerful healing ministry. All the world will know you!" The urge to comply with the suggestion was so great that it pulled at his entire being. Finally, deep down in the recesses of his soul a word formed—*Jesus*. He struggled to make his lips utter it—and at last he spoke aloud that name. The moment the word passed his lips, the vision of the beautiful figure disappeared from behind his closed eyelids.

The temptation to worship the powerful prince of this world (2 Cor. 4:4) is not to be taken lightly. The temptation to compromise—to pay homage to the world in order to gain a desirable end—is a subtle one and must be faced by each of us. Jesus told us, "No man can serve

IN THE FACE OF TEMPTATION

two masters'' (Matt. 6:24, KJV). Compromise is not possible in the realm of worship. To worship is to declare that God alone is worthy. To worship another creature or thing, in order to gain an end, is the very essence of rejecting God's throne rights.

Jesus' reply to the second temptation was, "It is written, 'You shall worship the Lord your God and serve Him only' '' (Luke 4:8). Again He referred to the Scripture record of the Israelites in the wilderness. They had been taught the same principle from Mount Sinai: "You shall have no other gods before Me" (Ex. 20:3).

Exposed to temptation when they no longer sensed God's presence with them, the Israelites disobeyed this command and worshipped the golden image of the calf. Again, where they failed and lost their provision, Jesus obeyed God's Word and won.

A Deadly Dare

Finally, Satan tried a third time, appealing to Jesus through His *imagination*, goading His pride, vanity and ego. Using a quotation from the Scriptures (Ps. 91:11) he posed the religious question:

And he led Him to Jerusalem and set Him on the pinnacle of the temple, and said to Him, "If You are the Son of God, cast Yourself down from here; for it is written, 'He will give His angels charge concerning You to guard You,' and 'On their hands they will bear You up, lest You strike Your foot against a stone.' '' And Jesus answered and said to him, "It is said, 'You shall not force a test on the Lord your God' '' (Luke 4:9-12).

We note that Satan took his scriptural reference out of context. This is perhaps the most dangerous form of temptation for a sincere Christian—the suggestion that there is scriptural authority for the proposed action. Satan suggested to Jesus that He do something spectacular to demonstrate His supernatural power. Miracles were to be a part of His ministry. To jump off the temple roof and be carried to the pavement below by God's angels could certainly launch His mission in a spectacular way.

What was wrong with the suggestion? Wasn't it true that God had promised to give His angels charge over Jesus? Wouldn't His jump demonstrate the glory and power of God to the people of Jerusalem?

First, consider the suggested action: to jump off the temple roof. It was spectacular, unusual, unnatural—and quite unnecessary. God seldom works in spectacular, unusual ways—and never in unnatural or unnecessary ways. When Jesus fed the 5,000, He didn't do it in a spectacular or unnatural way. Instead He quietly took the loaves and fishes, thanked God for them, and proceeded to divide them among the hungry. The whole process appeared so natural and simple that those who watched hardly realized a miracle was taking place.

Those who have witnessed or experienced physical healings often express amazement at how natural and simple the whole process appears to be. Two testimonies show this to be true. First is a woman who had suffered many years with crippling arthritis; second is a woman who was born nearly sightless.

"I had prayed for God to heal me and knew that in His great love, He would. One afternoon I was home alone, rejoicing in His love and concern. Suddenly my hands simply straightened out. All pain vanished, and before my eyes my fingers relaxed and looked and felt as if I had never had any discomfort or disease. It all happened so *naturally* that I caught myself thinking that the years of sickness had never been. I had expected God to heal in a more spectacular way.''

''I wanted to serve God as a Christian teacher and I knew I could serve Him better as a ''seeing'' teacher than a blind one. Finally, I got up the courage to ask God to heal me. I went to bed that night after praying and put my glasses on the nightstand. Next morning, I thought the sunshine seemed unusually bright, and the tree outside my window greener than before. I put on my glasses, as I always do first thing in the morning. To my surprise, everything looked fuzzy. Taking them off again, everything was clear! God had simply healed my sight while I slept. Being healed was the most *normal* thing I ever experienced.''

We are naturally drawn to the spectacular. Violence and drama occupy center stage in the secular world. Christians are drawn, too, toward the spectacular in demonstrations of God's power. This is how sincere believers are drawn into fanaticism of one kind of another. Claiming isolated Scripture texts as God's direction for their action, they look for strange and unusual so-called miracles as signs of spirituality.

A woman who had recently experienced a fresh encounter with the Holy Spirit came to my office deeply concerned that she might have disobeyed God in a particular incident. She had been attending a funeral where she had nearly been overcome with an urge to jump up during the service and command the body in the casket to come back to life. She had resisted and now was tormented by guilt.

''Did I disobey God?'' she asked. ''Jesus raised the dead and the Bible tells us that we can do what He did.''

Christ in the Wilderness

God is able to raise the dead, even today. But He will not use a believer to perform such a miracle without solid preparation. A fundamental part of the preparation is familiarity with the entire Scripture. We need to know the broad sweep of God's program here on earth. He will never ask us to do anything that is out of line with His character and total thrust.

This new Christian, unfamiliar with the whole Scripture, was a prime target for the temptation to "jump off the Temple roof." We read together the record of Jesus' temptation and His reply, and she came to see some of the workings of the tempter.

Let me give several checkpoints to help recognize whether or not an urge to do something that appears "spiritual" comes from God or Satan or our own desires:

1. Is it in line with God's total program as revealed in the Scripture? Does it reflect God's character of love and justice?

2. Is it spectacular, unusual or unnatural? If so, be careful. God usually works in simple, natural and intelligible ways.

3. Has God prepared you for it? God doesn't act on the spur of the moment: His Word and intentions are unchanging and eternal. When God wants you to do something, He will prepare you over a period of time, through Scripture, circumstances and impressions. When the time for action comes, you will recognize that God has led you.

4. Is it necessary? This may seem to be a superfluous question, but the temptation to engage in unnecessary activities "for the Lord" is a common one.

Returning to Jesus and Satan on the temple roof, we

hear the reply to the third temptation, "You shall not force a test on the Lord your God." Again, Jesus refers to the scriptural record of the Israelites in the wilderness. They had been warned not to put God to a foolish test (Deut. 6:16). Again, the Israelites failed; they asked for a sign greater than He was pleased to give. They provoked Him and lost their provision.

Jesus was tempted in the same realms as the Israelites. Where they lost, He won. Throughout the temptations, He did what they had been instructed to do. He stood on the naked Word of God without the conscious awareness of God's presence. When we are tempted, we must do likewise.

The only way through the problem is total reliance on God and His Word. There can be no other assurance of help. God's Word is sufficient. It is, therefore, essential that we be sure of what God has told us in the first place. Nothing is more tragic than the Christian who stands on *a* word of God—taken out of context and twisted by the master deceiver.

Christ in Contrast to Adam

There is another factor that needs to be incorporated into our total picture: Jesus was the sinless Son of God. Christ's temptation was different from ours in that, being sinless, He did not have "original sin" or the lust that is within. The appeal inserted into His sensorium found no lining in which to land. All attempts by Satan to call up a wayward, willful or lawless spirit in our Lord were to no avail.

In contrast, this is not true of us. *Satanic appeal into our sensorium finds some internal desire to have, experience and enjoy what is being offered.* Our temptation, paralleling the Lord's, is different in that we must

Christi in the Wilderness

figure into our equation the Adam factor or the reality of a sinful nature.

Let's look at this difference between Jesus and the rest of humanity....

chapter nine

The Adam Factor, the Jesus Factor

Though the origin of evil is shrouded in mystery, the fruit and results of it certainly are not. To what depth can a human being fall? It is true that humanity did fall, but are we still falling?

Our challenge is to ascertain the vital issue of what is in us that makes us want to yield to temptation.

Note the wisdom of Proverbs 9:17. The context is an illicit sexual encounter, and Solomon says, "Stolen water is sweet; and bread eaten in secret is sweet." How profound is this perception—that even well water tastes better if it is stolen (and you don't get caught). The plain crust of the bread eaten in secret tastes sweet! Strange, isn't it? The forbidden, the risque, that which we should not do, becomes the very thing we want to do.

One day while teaching a class I said, "You may look in all the pockets of my coat, suit and trousers, but you may not look in my shirt pocket." I paused a minute and then continued, ''What is it that doesn't care about the other pockets, but wants desperately to look in the one pocket that's forbidden''?

It is sin which is inherent, indwelling, which is now in focus. Pollution which resides within verses the act or action which produces guilt. *Prior to the act the pollution resides.* David, after he had sinned, had a God-given revelation of the depth of the problem. ''I was brought forth in iniquity [lawlessness] and in sin my mother conceived me'' (Ps. 51:5). We are not studying sin, but trying to discover what it is that is in the lining of a sensorium that is so receptive to the temptations offered by Satan. Remember, James 1:14 suggests that temptation becomes a sin when I am drawn away by my own lust. A thousand ugly, vulgar or violent suggestions sweep through my person, but they are not sin. Jesus was tempted in all manner as we, yet without sin. Sin and transgression begin when the suggestion lodges with my sensorium, like a fertilized egg into the lining of the womb.

Suddenly the process begins which we have described previously, and a ''conception'' takes place. When that temptation comes to full term, there is a ''birth'' which is, in biblical paradox, death (James 1:15)!

Our Flesh

The Greek scholar William Barclay wrote a small book entitled *Flesh and Spirit*. In one section, called ''The Enemy in the Soul,'' he refers to the apostle Paul's unique Greek word *sarx*, which is translated ''flesh.'' Paul seems to see *sarx* as the ''supreme enemy in the warfare of the soul.'' Barclay gives several uses of the Greek word *sarx* (flesh).

1) The flesh is the great enemy of the good life,

and of the Christian life. It is this sarx which renders the law impotent (Rom. 8:3). That is to say, it is this sarx which is responsible for that ever-repeated human situation in which a man quite clearly knows what to do and is yet quite helpless to do it. In the sarx nothing good dwells (Rom. 7:18). If we take this as a general statement, then it is exactly here that we see the difference between soma and sarx, body and flesh. The body can become the instrument of the service and the glory of God; the flesh cannot. The body can be purified and even glorified; the flesh must be eliminated and eradicated. It is with the flesh that a man serves the law of sin (Rom. 7:25). It is the sarx which renders a man quite incapable of assimilating the teaching which he ought to be able to receive (1 Cor. 3:1-3). The sarx cannot please God (Rom. 8:8). Worse than that, the sarx is essentially hostile to God (Rom. 8:7). Jealousy and strife and bitterness are the proof that a man or a community is living in the sarx (1 Cor. 3:3).

2) What then is the flesh? Clearly the flesh is not the body. It is equally clear, if the thought of Paul is consistent, that the flesh is not the natural man, for Paul did say that the natural man, the unchristian man, the pagan man, need not necessarily be totally bad. Even in such a condition there are times when man can do by nature what the law requires, because the requirements of the law are written on his heart, and because even in such a condition man possesses conscience (Rom. 2:14,15). To conceive of the flesh as the lower nature is not entirely satisfactory. To do so implies

that there is in man a nature which is capable of goodness, just as there is a nature which is doomed to evil. The trouble about such a view is that the rot, in spite of all that we have said about the natural man, is all through human nature; the entire structure is tainted. It is entirely significant that Paul speaks of the *works* of the flesh and the *fruit* of the Spirit (Gal. 5:19,22). A *work* is something which a man produces for himself; a *fruit* is something which is produced by a power which he does not possess. Man cannot *make* fruit. That is to say, man can easily enough produce evil for himself, he cannot help doing so; but goodness has to be produced for him by a power which is not his power. The thrust is that, while the translation "the lower nature" frequently makes good sense, it does not go far enough.

The essence of the flesh is this. No army can invade a country from the sea unless it can obtain a bridgehead. Temptation would be powerless to affect man, unless there was some thing already in man to respond to temptation. Sin could gain no foothold in a man's mind and heart and soul and life unless there was an enemy within the gates who was willing to open the door to sin. The flesh is exactly the bridgehead through which sin invades the human personality. The flesh is like the enemy within the gates who opens the way to the enemy who is pressing in through the gates.

But where does this bridgehead come from? Where does this enemy within spring from? It is the universal experience of life that a man by his conduct fits or unfits himself to receive any experience. He makes himself such that he will or will not respond to certain experiences. The flesh is what man has made himself in contrast with man as God made him. The flesh is man as he has allowed himself to become in contrast with man as God meant him to be. The flesh stands for the total effect upon man of his own sin and of the sin of his fathers and of the sin of all men who have gone before him. The flesh is human nature as it has become through sin. Man's sin, his own sin and the sin of mankind, has, as it were, made him vulnerable to sin. It has made him fall even when he knew he was falling and even when he did not want to fall. It has made him such that he can neither avoid the fascination of sin nor resist the power of sin. The flesh stands for human nature weakened, vitiated, tainted by sin. The flesh is man as he is apart from Jesus Christ and his Spirit.

We have established that the *sarx*, in Pauline usage, is that which is *within*, that to which temptation appeals in order to open the door to sin. *Sarx* or flesh cannot be improved, changed or reformed; it must die. "Now those who belong to Christ Jesus have crucified the flesh (*sarx*) with its passions and desires" (Gal. 5:24).

Jesus' Flesh?

Let us reexamine that wilderness temptation of our Lord Jesus in this light. Though the temptation and the possibility of disobedience were real, Jesus, being sinless, did not have a *sarx* (fleshly, sinful nature) to which Satan could appeal. Tempted in all manner like as we, Jesus nevertheless was without sin. His temptation was indeed like ours, yet He was without the evil inclination.

Remember our distinction: *Trial* from God does not solicit to evil. *Temptation* from the enemy draws downward toward evil by appealing to "something within." The difference between the two, we have observed, is motive and effect, rather than the approach. God tries, but does not tempt to evil (James 1:13). Satan tempts by appealing directly to the flesh (*sarx*) that which has polluted within.

When temptation comes from without, it is probing, reaching, investigating, seeking to find that which is within. Christ, as a *sinless* being can be tempted from without, but has nothing within to which the temptation can appeal. A sinless being may be tempted, but He cannot tempt Himself (to do evil) for there is nothing within. Thus, James says simply, God is untemptable!"

Our place in this scheme of things must be very clear. When temptation to sin comes to us from without, it does have something from *within* to which it can appeal. The power of temptation is testimony to the validity of the Genesis account and an acknowledgment of our personal pollution given to us by Adam's transgression.

Temptation, as contrasted to a test, must kindle something from *within* for it to function. If the person being tempted has dealt biblically with the *sarx* within, he becomes "temptation-proof." We would hope to see the difference between being *untemptable* as a sinless being and *temptation-proof* as a mature Christian who has been conformed to the image of Jesus Christ. Notice in this regard, Jesus' clear statement that "the ruler of the world is coming, and he has nothing in me." A free translation of the original could read, No hold, no rights or no claim on me!

Once we have been infected with sin, we possess a

sarx. With it there comes a lust for life which is imprisoned within one's own self. Sin creates in us a desire to do only that which is self-fulfilling because sin makes us our own god (see Gen. 3:22). Hence, narcissism can be understood from the Genesis 3 narrative of the fall of mankind.

Redemption can come *only* from outside of this fall. God became human. The sinless Son of God came not to grasp, lust or desire but to do the will of the One who sent Him. That will, like the will of God for us, is clearly set out in the principles of the Scripture. Christ proclaimed that His purpose was to fulfill, not abrogate, God's law (see Matt. 5:17-19). This was carefully demonstrated in His wilderness temptation, when He stood in the principle of Deuteronomy 6 and 8 rather than yield to the temptation presented to Him.

Pleonexia

The redemptive process still leaves within us that which desires what is forbidden. Post-baptismal sin and overt failure of Christians give empirical evidence that this is so. Yet the apostle Paul says, "Those who belong to Christ Jesus have crucified the flesh with its passions and lusts" (Gal. 5:24).

There are two basic approaches to interpreting Scripture which leaves the ordinary believer in confusion. The first is the *affirmative*, which sees the completed work of Christ. These teach there is no struggle, no progressive holiness, but we have been made complete in Christ. The second is the *aspirational*, which teaches man's responsibility and involvement. Both, of course, are true. We are crucified with Christ, completed and affirmed. This is a positional truth. We are in the process of becoming "temptation-proof" by maturity, aspiring to be conformed to the image of Jesus Christ. Keeping these both in focus will allow us to deal realistically with temptation without negating the completed work of Jesus Christ in our redemption.

Let's venture now into a group of words that are both serious and significant if we hope to understand temptation thoroughly. They are desire, concupiscence, covet, envy, lust, jealousy, passion, appetite, craving, proclivity, urge, inclination, longing and related words. With clear biblical evidence, I'm lumping all these words into one Greek word which expresses the intent of them all when used in negative, excessive or unprincipled manner. The Greek word is *pleonexia*, a broad term that has helped me to understand what it is that is *in* me—the *sarx* which opens the castle from within.

Going back to James 1:14, "Each one is tempted when he is carried away and enticed by his own lust," we find one of the Greek words in the above category. Paul says, in dealing with the works of the flesh, "Now those who belong to Christ Jesus have crucified the flesh (*sarx*) with its passions and desires" (Gal. 5:24). It clearly is the flesh that possesses the *passions* and *desires*, two more words that come under the above category of *pleonexia*. Let's look at Genesis 3:6 to set the stage: Eve crossed the line from test to temptation when she "saw that the tree was good for food, and that it was a delight to the eyes, and that the tree was desirable to make one wise." This places the root of sin in desire. Desire cultivated by the senses (sensorium) until it produced the transgression. The beginning of all that we know about human sin, tragedy, disobedience and failure is initiated by *an uncontrolled and an illegal desire inflamed by the senses!*

Here we touch the very watershed of human experience. So persuasive is this word *pleonexia* that God makes it one of His ten direct commandments, "You shall not covet." A criminal judge of many years with much experience in human degradation said, "Of all the human emotions, my conviction is that jealousy is the most powerful of them all."

Let us study a more complete definition of *pleonexia*, whose root meaning is "to increase, then to take advantage, defraud or make gain by an illegal manner." Thus, in application, it means:

1. being ruthless, aggressive and self-assertive;

2. extending and maintaining one's self over others by strength;

3. the desire to steal;

4. an uncontrolled desire for advantage;

5. a desire which is excessive, inordinate and ungoverned, ruining human life;

6. an unrestrained sexual desire;

7. disorders of the human heart, closely allied to selfishness;

8. an almost irresistible desire to increase one's possessions;

9. in modern parlance, "to rip off";

10. a striving for unlawful wealth which leads to violence;

11. a malignant passion which is hard to cure;

12. to lose one's relationship to other things in his desire to acquire.

Robert Trench, in his book *Synonyms of the New Testament*, says *pleonexia* is the root from which the "love for money" (which is the root of all evil) is derived. But *pleonexia* is a wider and deeper word.

William Barclay, in *New Testament Wordbook*, says
"*Pleonexia* is an ugly word and always has a certain
basic idea behind it which none of the translations brings
out, because it cannot be done in one word. In classic
Greek it means 'an arrogant greediness.' "

This word relates to Satan, the tempter himself. John
10:10 says he is a thief who comes to steal, kill and
destroy. This is his nature, not just his activity. Other
scriptures describe him:

• 2 Corinthians 2:11: "In order that no advantage
(*pleonexia*) be taken of us by Satan." That is, his overreaching, grasping activity and disposition are ready,
always ready, to take advantage of us. "We are not [my,
how I wish this were so] ignorant of his schemes."

• Ephesians 4:27: "Do not give the devil an opportunity." The obvious meaning is that, due to his nature,
he is ready to take advantage of our anger and move in.

• 1 Corinthians 7:5: "Lest Satan tempt you because
of your lack of self-control." He is then pictured as
ready to "overreach" in a good marriage to tempt one
to adultery.

• 2 Corinthians 11:14: "Satan disguises himself as
an angel of light." The lesson is that he deceives, takes
advantage of and gains power over a person by disguis-
ing himself as a messenger of the God of light.

Application of Pleonexia

Anthony Hoekema, in his book *Created in God's
Image*, says, "We simply cannot understand *how* we
sinned in Adam, the Bible does not tell us. Nor can we
understand how the guilt of Adam's sin is imparted to
us; the Bible does not answer that question either. What
the Bible does tell us is *that* we sinned in Adam and
that the guilt of Adam's first sin remains a mystery,

not only in its commission but also in its transmission.''

Admitting the mystery and not trying empirically to prove all that I suggest, I'll proceed with the players on the stage: God, Satan, Adam and Eve and us. From Isaiah 14 and Ezekiel 38:28, most scholars accept that Satan is a created being, holding a high place in the economy of God. The New Testament says, ''He is a liar, and the father [originator] of lies'' (John 8:44) and that he ''[fell] from heaven like lightning'' (Luke 10:18). The ''I wills'' of Satan's boast in Isaiah 14 suggest to me that he was the father of *pleonexia* as well, desiring, coveting and overreaching what was not his appointed portion. If that kind of sin mysteriously originated in Satan, it does shed some light on the fall.

This father of lies and desire approached the innocent pair—Adam and Eve—in a beguiling form, asking the religious question, ''Has God actually said?'' Eve's response was not one of rebellion, anger or even self-will, but one of inflamed desire (*pleonexia*). When she finally acted, as did Adam, it was forcibly motivated by lust (craving for that which is beyond limits). In the transgression of God's principle and the consequent fall, original sin came into the human race. And the pollution of sin (innate, inward, pervasive, depravity) took—and takes—the form of *pleonexia*, similar to or infected by the nature of Satan: an uncontrolled desire for advantage.

The desire leads to action, which takes the form of *anomia* (guilt), resulting in lawlessness, rebellion and self-will. *Sarx*, the New Testament term, describes the ethical and moral effect of the fall in all mankind. In the *sarx* dwells no good thing—but pollution (*pleonexia*) and guilt (*anomia*).

If, indeed, *pleonexia* dwells in the *sarx* as the apostle Paul states in Galatians 5:24, we can begin to see our own lust upon which Satan draws in the time of temptation.

The lining of the sensorium which Satan can approach so easily is the *pleonexia*, the desire for what is forbidden. This is what we have as sinners, which Christ did not have being sinless.

If the sinful nature is basically *pleonexia*, it helps explain a thousand things:

Why the children of Israel thought leeks and onions preferable to God's shekinah glory and the Promised Land. Why a simple thing like water in the desert could become a source of shame, resulting in their tempting God. Why meat was such an issue as to cause them to be judged and to suffer leanness of soul. Why Esau would trade his whole future for a bowl of lentils. Why the wife of the businessman in Proverbs 7:6-23 searches for the young man. Why Judas kept stealing from the money bag and sold his Master for thirty pieces of silver. Why Demas could love this present world enough to forsake his call.

On what principle does the "con" man work? He appeals to our greed and we are taken. How does a salesman get you to sign an order? By appealing to your very own *pleonexia* which you received from Adam. It is clear to me that a study of the "works of the flesh," such as William Barclay's *Flesh and Spirit*, would reveal that most, if not all, of the fifteen Greek words Paul used to describe the "works of the flesh" in Galatians 5 would be rooted in or applied to *pleonexia*. It really is an ugly word, as the Greek scholars suggested! It speaks of unlawful desire or lawlessness and greed—in short, sin.

Temptation, then, works when my inflamed greed within thinks it has found a short cut or can take advantage of another to satisfy my own needs and wants. Reduced to that kind of language it is ugly, and, as we face it, the truth will set us free.

Abiding in Jesus

Jesus knows clearly what the issues are: "For we do not have a high priest who cannot sympathize with our weakness [Adamic nature], but one who has been tempted in all things as we are, yet without sin" (Heb. 4:15). In light of this, we are encouraged to come boldly to the throne and boldly expect mercy and grace, in the time of need!

Thus, He invites us to continue with Him in His temptation. We know that He is with us in our temptation, but are we going with Him in His? Abiding, according to John 15, is the key to all of God's provision. Abiding means staying with Him through the hard and difficult times. John 6:66 refers to a day after which "many of his disciples went back, and walked no more with him" (KJV). *Out of our temptation into participation in His is the route to spiritual maturity* (see Luke 22:28,29).

When Satan left Jesus in the wilderness, God sent angels to care for Him. This strengthens the fact that Jesus was in the wilderness without a sense of the presence of God. When the angels came to care for Him, the sense of God's concern, love and presence returned. Then "Jesus returned to Galilee in the power of the Spirit" (Luke 4:14).

Compare this statement with the one made before the wilderness experience (Luke 4:1). After the testing in the wilderness, Jesus was full of the Holy Spirit's *power*. Now He was ready to enter into the provision—the ministry God had prepared for Him. Jesus was on the victory side of the problem and He could announce to the world that He had come to fulfill what the Scripture promised (Luke 4:16-21). Here is a portion of His statement:

> "The Spirit of the Lord is upon Me, because He anointed Me to preach the gospel to the poor. He has sent Me to proclaim release to the captives, and recovery of sight to the blind, to set free those who are downtrodden, to proclaim the favorable year of the Lord" (Luke 4:18,19).

We have reason to look at the church today and ask, "Where is the power Jesus promised the believers? Where is the ability to meet the need of the oppressed, the sick, the blind and the brokenhearted?

Power as a promise isn't the same as power in action! Between the promise and the realization of power come the principle and the problem. Victory in the problem transforms the promise into power.

Ultimately, the goal is not only personal triumph over sin, but the joining of our resources with our Master to see His triumph over the powers and forces of hell. We begin to take up His burden for the nations, feel His passion for the sick, the lost and the oppressed.

Jesus, remember, suffered temptation not for Himself. He had not sinned, but His life was spent for others, particularly for you and me. When that sinks in, we find ourselves debtors, struggling to find out how we can more effectively be involved with bringing that redemption to others. This search helps us to find and face some *real* temptations. For this is the kind of temptation that comes to the man or woman who wants to live godly, be useful and declare the message of release to all who will listen (see Phil. 1:29).

As we mature, there is a realm where we can increasingly touch what God wants to do in us for others. Being done with lesser things, we sense the excitement of destiny and purpose. In a sense the Master's whole life was a season of temptation, reproach, indignities and mockeries. The enemy mocked Him, accused Him of illegitimacy, of being a glutton and a wine-drinker, the chief of the demons, seditious and seeking to break the law of Moses.

How does this affect us? Peter hit it squarely when he said, ''Since Christ has suffered in the flesh, arm yourselves also with the same purpose, because he who has suffered in the flesh has ceased from sin'' (1 Pet. 4:1). He means, let us step out of the personal arena and find Christ's purpose and vision or direction, for some suffering keeps us from involvement in things that are sinful! Peter continues, saying that we no longer live for the lusts of man, ''but for the will of God'' (v. 2). Later he says, ''Do not be surprised at the fiery ordeal...which comes upon you for your testing [temptation, same word in Greek, remember], as though some strange thing were happening to you; but to the degree that you share the sufferings of Christ, keep on rejoicing'' (vv. 12,13). Peter takes it out of the realms of the ''puddle'' experience and sets us, when ready, into the cosmic excitement of Christ's eternal purpose.

The Ultimate Temptation

The ultimate display of the power of temptation and its defeat is in the Garden of Gethsemane. This test was from God; the temptation was from Satan. Over the soul and spirit of the Son of God swept a depth of human passion and suffering never to be duplicated. It seems as if Satan sought to crush what he could not capture.

Let's see if promise, principle, problem and provision stand as God's way of working when the eternal dealing of mankind rests on the outcome. The *promise*, I would suggest, is found in Isaiah 53:11: Jesus would see the fruit of the anguish of His soul and be satisfied! The *principle* is found in Psalm 40:7,8: "In the scroll of the book it is written of me; I delight to do Thy will, O my God; Thy law is within my heart." Then came the *problem*.

He who knew no sin was about to be made sin and the sheer contradiction of it all was overwhelming. His human pain in finding His followers asleep is real and touching. The magnitude of what was being asked broke upon Him, perhaps as it did upon Abraham when he realized that God was asking for him to give up Isaac. The demand—to be made sin—must be beyond the call of duty. Jesus' mind cast about for an alternate route. (Options are not rebellion nor are they refusal.) "Father, if Thou art willing, remove this cup from Me; yet not My will, but Thine be done" (Luke 22:42).

We have repeatedly suggested that in the temptation itself, withdrawal of the *sense* of God's presence presses us into the principle and out of the sense realm. Then the Word searches us out, pressing us to the razor's edge to bring forth obedience based on the power of His Word. When the test comes, the teacher doesn't talk. In this instance, angels came to minister and to strengthen Jesus (Luke 22:43).

But there comes, not through clenched teeth nor a reluctant heart, a victorious response, "My Father, if this cannot pass away unless I drink it, Thy will be done" (Matt. 26:42).

There must not, indeed there cannot, now be an illegal desire nor a propensity in the heart of the Son of God to take a short cut. To do so would speak confusion into the eternal redemptive process. Rather there is demonstrated an ultimate clinging to God, to His Person, to His faithfulness and above all to His eternal Word. The ultimate religious question is now being asked here in Gethsemane: ''Did God really require this of You?''

In his book *The Lord*, Romano Guardini discusses something of the issues in the problem:

Who knows how God the Father faced his Son in that hour? He never ceased to be his Father; the band of endless love between them which is the Spirit never broke; and yet—''My God, my God, why hast thou forsaken me?'' (Matt. 27:46). If we do not prefer to pass over this in reverent silence, we must say that God permitted his Son to taste the human agony of rejection and plunge towards the abyss. Christ's terrible cry from the cross came from the bitter dregs of the consequence of his union with us. But the chalice was given him to taste already in Gethsemane, when, his consciousness of the abysmal forlornness of the world heightened by God's proximity, his Father began to ''withdraw'' from him. It was then that Jesus' knowledge and suffering reached the frightful intensity evidenced by his terror, agonized praying, and sweat of blood that streamed to the ground. In much the same way, a whirlpool on the surface of an ocean may be the visible sign of a catastrophe at its depths surpassing imagination.

Into the problem comes the pain of crucifixion and

Jesus' heightened sense of abandonment. Then He surrendered His life. John records Jesus as saying that "the Father loves Me, because I lay down My life that I may take it again. No one has taken it away from Me, but I lay it down on My own initiative" (John 10:17,18). He surrendered His life but held fast to his obedience. He died with a broken heart, but His human will was confident and trusting.

Into the grave went an apparently defeated, unmercifully lacerated human body. There it lay for three days and nights, while the forces of hell rejoiced. But their rejoicing was short-lived. They failed to consider the exceedingly powerful provision. "Blessed is a man who perseveres under trial; for once he has been approved, he will receive the crown of life, which the Lord promised to those who love Him" (James 1:12).

The provision was described in detail in the Psalms years before. Listen to the *provision*, for it directly affects you.

This Man, delivered up by the predetermined plan and foreknowledge of God, you nailed to a cross by the hands of godless men and put Him to death. And God raised Him up again, putting an end to the agony of death, since it was impossible for Him to be held in its power. For David says of Him, "I was always beholding the Lord in my presence; for He is at my right hand, that I may not be shaken. Therefore my heart was glad and my tongue exulted; moreover my flesh also will abide in hope; because Thou wilt not abandon my soul to Hades, nor allow Thy Holy One to undergo decay. Thou hast made known to me the ways of life; Thou wilt make me full of gladness with Thy presence'' (Acts 2:23-28).

Yes, this Son of Man shall see the travail of His soul and be satisfied. God would not, He could not, leave His soul in Hades. The provision is as sure as the promise to the one who understands!

If the church today lacks power, it isn't because God has withheld His promise or broken His Word, but because there are so few Christians who have come through the problem successfully. The power promised to the church is dissipated by repeated laps around the mountain.

Jesus withstood the temptations in the wilderness. He withstood the temptation at Gethsemane. He died and rose again, and because He did, the way is open for us to withstand. We, too, can stand on the principle of God's naked Word and be prepared to receive the fullness of the power of the Holy Spirit. This power is promised to us, as believers, not in our strength, but in His!

chapter ten

Teach Us, Lord

Temptation serves the purpose of exposing what is really in our hearts. This is necessary before we can have an honest and satisfactory relationship with God—and reach the maturity by which we enter into the provisions of the promised land.

Lead Us Not Into Temptation

In answer to a request for a lesson in prayer, Jesus taught His disciples, "Do not lead us into temptation, but deliver us from evil" (Matt. 6:13). Some theologians have questioned whether or not this verse belongs in the Bible. They are of the opinion that God doesn't lead anyone into temptation, and to ask Him not to do it clearly implies that He might possibly do it.

Let us grasp three possible meanings of this prayer ("Lead us not into temptation") and then make some general application.

First, as H.A.W. Meyer said in his *Commentary on*

IN THE FACE OF TEMPTATION

Matthew, "God leads us into temptation insofar as, in
the course of His administration, He brings about a state
of things that lead to temptation, that is, the situations
that furnish an occasion for sinning; and therefore, if
a man happens to encounter such dangers to his soul,
it is caused by God—it is He who does it. This is different from the inward temptation described by James.
The active force in that temptation is not of God, but
man's own lusts, and that in consequences of his *sarx*
(flesh)."

Meyer is pointing out the difference between trial and
temptation. We know, as Jesus knew, that in the trial
(hurricane) was the temptation (tornados) which caused
the damage.

A second opinion is presented by Rudolph Steir in
his book *The Words of Jesus*:

But how does the Lord ascribe temptation to the
Father, who tempteth no man to evil? Partly
because all things which may befall us are under
His dominion and permission, and then because
He would have the uncontested right to permit our
falling, to subject us to tests which we could not
sustain, and trials in which we could not stand. This
right we humbly concede to His justice; but know
that, while we ask according to His command and
promise, His mercy, the same which forgave our
sin, will not leave us to our corruption, to contract
fresh guilt.

This argument comes from God's sovereignty and is
certainly a valid insight and application. That God has
the right and privilege to lead us into temptation cannot be questioned. That this will issue into something
redemptive and not a solicitation to evil has been settled.

Third, this may be a prayer for God's intervention that temptation would not come too soon and be too strong. That temptation *will* come is a given conclusion. This prayer then would go something like this, "While the persecuted are blessed, and Christ rewards a heroic and determined attitude, we are all not there yet." This interpretation implies that the Lord's prayer not to be led into temptation is not merely for the heroes, but for the timid, the inexperienced. We can request that the teacher be considerate and allow time for reaching the heights of heroism on which James stood when he wrote, "Consider it all joy...when you encounter various trials" (James 1:2).

We have then truth in tension. We can pray with real fervency not to be led into temptation, especially if we recognize that ultimately temptations are necessary. But when trial/temptation comes our attitude should change immediately. We should recognize it as being sovereignly allowed. The mental attitude should be, "God has allowed this. It is the battle for which I have been trained by His love and Word. By His grace, I'll enter with joy, believing the temptation itself will be an arena whereby I can demonstrate my faithfulness to Him and to His Word." This is not done in triumphalism or self-confidence, but rather in a cautious humility mixed with a sense of Christ's ultimate victory. We know by our study of temptation that all must be tested, so we must not run, hide nor shrink from the responsibility.

The wire is stretched across the gorge on Niagara Falls. The man will ride a bicycle across the wire. He asks you, "Do you think I can do it?" "Yes," you reply with eagerness, "you can do it!"

"Great," he answers, "get on the handle bars."

As a hush goes over the crowd, you remember that in the test the teacher gets quiet and will refuse to answer any questions, unless they are in the realm of procedure or perhaps a point of clarification. A test is a test, and strangely enough, it *is* for your benefit. It is test/temptation that shows us our weakness, tries our faith, promotes humility and teaches us a genuine dependence on God.

Five School Lessons

In one sense I see every Christian as a student in the school of temptation, where we are to learn five lessons.

1. *All temptation is rooted in the appeal to appetites, desires and impulses.* There are only a few absolutes in dealing with the human predicament; this, I believe, is one of them: Every temptation is made real by offering the person some seeming advantage. This is the illegal desire to satisfy some inflamed desire whether material, sexual or sensual. This we have described as *pleonexia* and it is rooted in the flesh.

2. *Once the desire is inflamed there follows the necessity of finding the short cut.* Lawlessness is substituting God's known will with plans of my own. Once I see what I want, the mechanism of how to get it is put into gear.

The "short cut" is a graphic illustration of lawlessness. In a foot race, you are required to finish the course on the track. The person who wants to get to the finish line ahead of the others has two choices, run faster or cut across the middle grass. The judges, of course, see the short cut and disqualify the runner.

What may be worse is if the cheating runner *not* be seen, then take the prize and allow everyone to think he is the fastest runner. Thus, he *thinks* he has fooled everyone: God, the committee, the school and, of course, his family.

There is one verse that should put the fear of God in us all, demanding that we never, never take the short cut however badly we desire (*pleonexia*) the prize: "Because the sentence against an evil deed is not executed quickly, therefore the hearts of the sons of men among them are given fully to do evil" (Eccl. 8:11). Because God often waits until evil matures and becomes full before He executes judgment, men misunderstand His slowness to judge to be His failure or reluctance to do so. This is a costly, if not fatal, assumption. (Compare 2 Pet. 3:4-9.)

The one who misinterprets God's slowness to judge and thus gives himself to greed and shortcuts is heading toward the proverbial "brick wall" of God's inevitable and consequential judgment.

As an old Christian master of the ways of God says, "God's judgments have leaden heels, but iron hands!"

3. *The "fiery darts" are powerful.* Paul, in his teaching on spiritual warfare, teaches us about "inflamed missiles." We must know how the "fiery darts" work as well as acknowledge their existence. On the *occasion* of temptation, they attack the mind suddenly and with a kind of bombardment. In the *hour* of temptation, they work like a low-grade infection, repeatedly waiting to be entertained, accepted and received. In the much longer *season* of temptation, the darts are like radiation. They are continuous, unrelenting and designed to wear you down, wear you out and leave you in despair, depressed or suicidal.

The object of the fiery dart is to inflame the emotions and/or the reason. It looks something like this:

Emotion = what I feel

Reason = what I think

} these two move the human will to action

If the first dart lodges in the emotions, it makes what I feel to be the law of action, rather than God's Word. All of this begins in the sensorium because when I yield to "what I feel," it changes or affects "what I think." Actually, it causes me to begin to think differently from the Word of God. Now I am responding to the religious question. An illustration will help. "You don't feel very 'Christian' today, do you?" comes the fiery dart to the emotions. The mind agrees, "You haven't acted very Christian in the past three weeks." Now, into the senses wherein dwells the flesh, enters the satanic suggestion, ever so gentle, ever so clever and very deceitful. The reason, or mind, is not subject to the law of God (see Rom. 8:6,7), and it joins in the battle against you. When the emotions and the mind agree, they have the ability to move the human will. "You're right," they all agree, "let's go have a drink. You can't live this Christian life anyhow." Now the will sets the agenda for action, which is lawlessness, that is, substituting my own evaluation of the program for God's clear Word. What I feel and what I think becomes the determinative force. Self is deified, becoming God in the situation.

4. *The measure of the severity of God's dealing is directly proportionate to the depth of the habit patterns engraved in my personality.* Some people are, by temperament, more easily taught than others. Some, it seems, need to be hit with a coal shovel just to get their attention. Isaiah 28:28 gives us a beautiful and

comforting insight into the fatherhood of God. ''Grain for bread is crushed, Indeed, he does not continue to thresh it forever. Because the wheel of his cart and his horses eventually damage it, he does not thresh it longer.'' The lesson may not be obvious, but he says, in beautiful ''farmer language,'' that God never, never uses more force than necessary to crush the grain He needs in order to feed the hungry soul and spirit. If you are in severe temptation, spend time in this passage. Our Father, in order to change deeply ingrained and sometimes stubborn habit patterns, will not use more force than is needed. (I should know.) Don't run from Him; run into Him for discipline and comfort.

When testing and temptation seem severe, you must begin to respond to God, who has been forced to ''turn up the heat'' to get you out of the cyclical take-another-lap into the linear movement toward spiritual maturity and progress. Failure to respond to the depth of God's dealings sets us up for bleached bones, that is, a premature physical death. This is not, as I said before, necessarily an eternal loss of one's salvation but a judgment clearly demonstrated in Exodus, repeated for New Testament Christians in 1 Corinthians 10.

5. *We must not impeach ourselves.* When the apostle Paul described what we have called the promised land, he asks this question, ''Who shall impeach those whom God has chosen? Will God Himself impeach them? Why, He declares them free from guilt! Who is there to condemn them? Will Christ Jesus condemn them? Why, He died for them!'' (Rom. 8:33,34, Weymouth). God reveals to us the nature of our own selfishness, pollution and greed, and such revelation seems more than we can bear, and the danger is twofold.

First, we tend to surmise that the revelation is a surprise to God. No, He knew it when He called us. "While you were yet a sinner, Christ died for you" (see Rom. 5:6).

The second danger is more alarming. No one, I repeat, no one can impeach you—have you removed from your place and calling as a Christian. Not God, for the reasons given. Not Christ, as He provided salvation for you. Not Satan nor things present nor things to come nor people, though they may try, for it is God who justifies. Then where lies the danger? It lies in self-impeachment. The believer who has repeatedly yielded to temptation (it seems as if self-impeachment is more likely to occur in a long season of temptation rather than a more confined occasion or an hour) may begin the impeachment proceedings. Agreeing with the accuser, against God and His Word, is to "[make] Him a liar, because he has not believed in the witness that God has borne concerning His Son" (1 John 5:10).

When I pastored in the late sixties, I had a parishioner whom I came to appreciate and admire. She was hungry for God and became an intercessor for our family and my ministry. Once, in a large evangelistic meeting, this lady was identified by the evangelist by her dress and hair color. Asked to stand, she did so timidly, unaware of what was to happen. In what would be an unbiblical use of personal prophecy, he said to her, "You are hypocritical and full of pride." It was false, untrue and very damaging. I came to know her family, her love for God and the time she spent in the Scripture and in prayer. This was not only a fiery dart, but it was also the beginning of what I see as the self-impeachment process.

She never did get free from the accusation. It has followed her through all of her Christian experience. All the reassurance, ministry and scriptural evidence could never permanently penetrate that self-impeachment. Though all the powers of hell could not touch her, she seemingly could not help herself in continually condemning and accusing her own self, after all, "It was a man of God who said it." In one sense she verged on tempting God, for she refused to believe what He had said. Our inflamed emotions can trap us into the realm of temptation whereby "what I feel" and "what I think" take a very real precedence over what God has said.

Deliver Us From Evil

This, the seventh petition in the Lord's Prayer, puts the goal of temptation squarely into focus. That we are taught to pray to be delivered from evil certainly gives us the sense and hope that this prayer can and should be answered. The prayer suggests that this evil or the evil one (Satan) should not be able to harm the soul of the godly person.

Though the prayer "Lead us not into temptation" is valid, all temptation cannot be avoided. In the on-going sovereignty of God, we are involved and exposed to some temptation. So it is with evil. We can be delivered from that which is harmful to the soul, but not always can we be totally free from the all-persuasive presence of evil that John describes. "The whole world lies in the power of the evil one" (1 John 5:19). Let's set some guidelines in order to understand how this prayer for deliverance is to be answered.

Before the death of our Lord Jesus, the devil exhibited a strange power over mankind. But the power of Christ's kingdom and His redemptive death broke Satan's hold once and for all. Those who are "in Christ" have been and can be victorious over Satan and reign as kings in this life.

Presupposing that you are "in Christ," what must you know for this prayer ("Deliver us from evil") to be answered? Since it is a promise, it must have certain conditions (principles). Those principles will be tested (problem), and those people who walk out of the problem will enter the provision—deliverance from evil!

St. Cyril, one of the ante-Nicene fathers of the church, made this mature observation and comment:

Temptation is like a winter torrent, difficult to cross. Some, being most skillful swimmers, pass over, not being whelmed beneath temptations, nor swept down by them all, while others, who are not such, entering into them, sink in them. As an example, Judas, entering into the temptation of covetousness, swam not through it, but, sinking beneath it, was choked both in body and spirit. Peter entered into the temptation of the denial, but having entered it, he was not overwhelmed by it, but manfully swimming through it, *he was delivered* (italics mine).

Many people see God as rescuer; we pray and He rescues, again and again. But closer reading of the Scriptures will help you see that God is an enabler rather than a rescuer. He will rescue in certain emergency situations (Peter sinking in the waves [Matt. 14:30], for example). Ordinarily He looks for ways that He can strengthen you and cause you to use the weapons He has provided to enable you to stand (see Eph. 6:10-14). Failing to know the nature of warfare, refusing to grow up and otherwise revolting against maturity does not make you safer but exposes you to painful failure. The Bible is full of such examples and there are many around you. Again, one of the early church fathers, St. Basil, wisely speaks,

> Many who have laid up much spiritual wealth from their youth, and have arrived at middle age, when temptations arise against them by the machinations of the evil one, have not succeeded in resisting the weight of the tempest, but have lost all. Some concerning faith have made shipwreck; others have cast away the chastity treasured from youth under some sudden hurricane of sinful pleasure which has rushed upon them. A most piteous spectacle that a man, after self-denial, after fasting, after long prayer, after plentiful tears, after twenty or thirty years' devotedness, a man should, through an unwatchful spirit and carelessness, be made a show of, and stripped of all!

It is interesting in this same light that St. Augustine prayed that his heart (desires) and the presence of temptation would not meet at the same time!

One clear goal of the whole Bible seems to me to be the process of making the serious and mature child of God to be *temptation-proof*. I am not saying that Christians come to the place where, as God has described in James 1:13, we are untemptable. Neither do I hold some latent form of perfectionism. I do know that growth, maturity, repeated testing and victories remove, in a progressive manner, our "temptableness."

Let me explain. Temptation and trial develop our endurance and Christian character, so that we are "perfect and complete, lacking nothing" (James 1:4). The same teaching is given several places in the New

Testament, particularly in Romans 5:1-5 and 1 Peter 1:6,7. And the writer to the Hebrews says, "Who because of practice [in testing and temptation] have their senses trained to discern good and evil" (5:14). (This, by the way, is the same phrase used to describe the tree of the knowledge of good and evil, in the garden.) Thus, the process of maturity is seen as progressively becoming more Christ-like. And Christ "learned obedience from the things which He suffered" (Heb. 5:8). This was not in relation to sin, because He was and is sinless. Our testing, temptation and suffering then can take on a different meaning other than continually struggling with sexual impulses or wanting to quit being a Christian because it doesn't go the way we thought it should.

Jesus' obedience, life, discernment, image and love for God's law must be, indeed can be, worked in us. We can come to a matured perception of what is good (beneficial) and evil (harmful in God's sight) in a manner that could not be demanded of a new believer with biblical illiteracy and inexperience.

Let us press the distinction now between being *untemptable* as God is and coming to be *temptation-proof.* This must be made clear so that God can answer our prayers to be delivered from evil. The person who has understood by revelation and painful human experience the reality of the fall and his or her all-pervasive polluted nature is driven to Christ for redemption. He or she is born again, and in-dwelt by the Spirit of Christ (see Rom. 8:9). By virtue of that indwelling nature, a person comes increasingly to love righteousness and hate lawlessness (see Heb. 1:9). Thus, God is bringing him or her to the razor's edge, making a separation between good and evil. Progressively, this Christian's confidence grows in the reliability of God's law. He or she has believed it, but now is learning to live by it and beginning to enjoy the freedom of living by God's revelations as contrasted to the bondage of having to figure everything out on one's own (see John 8:31,32). These laws are now being written on the Christian's heart by the Holy Spirit (2 Cor. 3:3) and, by reason of testings and temptation in daily life, he or she can discern between good and evil.

Let us take this person back into the garden, in the presence of the tree of the knowledge of good and evil and reenact the first temptation. Without being childish or theatrical, I can picture how this mature and war-weary soldier of Christ would respond. He or she is not now innocent but righteous. Not naive but as harmless as a dove. Not childish but childlike, having come to a real dependency on God and His Word. By virtue of repeated failure and God's grace which has been sufficient, this Christian has learned a few things.

The serpent slithers through the branches and asks his religious question, "Has God really said? Go ahead, you will not die!" The soldier breaks into a controlled laughter. The line sounds so familiar. Experience in temptation enables Christian to smell death in the air. Knowing that he barely conquered death through the enabling and imparted power of the risen Lord, our soldier responds, "No thanks, if anyone knows God's *promises*, I do. God, in Christ, has carefully taught me His *principles*. By His grace and in His name, I am going to abide in what He said, even if it means my life. There is no *need* that I could imagine nor any *desire* so strong that it would be worth trading what God has done for me. I would rather deny my actual need than attempt to supply it illegally, for I *know* that leads to death."

Christian then, in holy anger, addresses rather than simply resists Satan because what is actually taking place is so clearly seen. "Be gone, Satan! For it is written, You shall worship the Lord your God, and serve Him only" (Matt. 4:10).

I trust you see the important difference between being untemptable and having arrived at a place of maturity where you have been delivered from the evil one! In the above illustration, we can say that Christian matured through testing to become temptation-proof. This in no way denies the admonition of 1 Corinthians 10:12: "Therefore let him who thinks he stands take heed lest he fall." This is a clear warning regarding overconfidence and presumption. These two accusations could not be applied to our battle-wise spiritual veteran.

A Final Word

One last lesson—from Simon Peter. Before His trial Jesus says quite abruptly and very directly, "Simon, Satan has demanded permission to sift you like wheat." Because our Lord is an enabler, not primarily a rescuer, He added, "I have prayed for you, that your faith may not fail" (Luke 22:31,32). This indicates that when faith is in place, temptation is weakened.

As overconfident and brash as Peter was, he was sifted! After failure, fear, cursing, backsliding and leading other disciples off, he was restored. (Peter's story may indicate that a direct "roaring-lion" attack may be more easily defeated than a subtle, quiet erosion like the one that overcame Judas Iscariot.)

Eventually Peter became an instructor in the school of temptation. In his epistles he gave lessons on how not to stumble.

In his second epistle Peter gives nine principles that build upon each other to make us temptation-proof.

1. *Diligence:* Be persistent, stick to it, work at it. And remember, it isn't our *own* work, but rather persistence in clinging to Christ who works *in* us. Use your diligence to exercise faith.

2. *Faith:* Employ every effort to exercise your faith. Settle in your heart the essence of faith as given to us in Hebrews 11:1: "Now faith is the assurance (the confirmation, the title-deed) of the things [we] hope for, being the proof of things [we] do not see and the conviction of their reality—faith perceiving as real fact what is not revealed to the senses" (Amplified).

Faith exercised will develop in you moral excellence.

3. *Moral excellence:* That means doing it right. Don't take the short cut! Practice it to develop knowledge.

4. *Knowledge:* Learn to know God better and discover what He wants you to do. Seek out His will for you. Study your Bible. Don't spend your life being spoon-fed by others. Get a good Bible dictionary and learn how to use a concordance. Grow up in your personal knowledge of God, His ways and His Word. In practicing what you know about God's ways, develop self-control.

5. *Self-control:* This is a difficult one! Have you ever promised you won't get mad again? You make this promise to your wife and she reminds you sweetly, "But, honey, you always lose your temper." To which you flare back, "Well, I said I wouldn't do it anymore!"

What causes us to lose control? Our stubborn self-wills. We get mad when our wills are opposed, our comfort disturbed, our opinions questioned. The problem is always our giant-sized egos. How can we practice self-control? Not by gritting our teeth and saying, ''I won't get mad. I won't get mad.'' Self will be controlled when we put aside our desires, die to our egos and let Jesus control us. When our self is controlled by Him, we have learned the real meaning of the word self-control. When this happens, you will develop perseverance.

6. *Perseverance:* This is steadfast endurance in all circumstances and only develops as it is practiced. Perseverance comes only when you turn your preferences over to Jesus. He is able to reign in all circumstances of life; and when you let Him control you, you will begin to partake of the divine nature and the divine patience. Practicing steadfast perseverance leads to godliness.

7. *Godliness:* This is a word with many implications. An important one is impartiality or justice. God is totally just and impartial. You can measure your godliness by the way you treat your enemies. Do you love them as you do your friends? If you were God and had some rain to give, on whom would you send it? The just *and* the unjust? The ability to be impartial is a mark of godliness. As you practice godliness, you develop brotherly kindness,

8. *Brotherly kindness:* Can you look at every person with compassion? Even if he or she is dirty, ugly or mean? Brotherly kindness is part of the provision God has made for us. Put aside the old reactions to people you dislike. Yield yourself to Christ and let His affection come through you. Practicing brotherly kindness will develop Christian love.

9. *Christian love:* Christian love is *agape*, the highest

form of love—a reasoning, intentional, deliberate, spiritual devotion for someone. This is not an emotional feeling—variable as the wind—but a steady, unchanging affection.

The natural love most of us humans are capable of is always directed toward something or someone we like, are attracted to and approve. *Agape* is the nature of God's love. He loves us when we are ugly, wrong and rebellious. Admittedly, it is impossible for us to love like that unless Christ lives and loves in us. With His love in us, we can will to love as God directs us, regardless of our feelings.

When we find ourselves confronted with someone we don't feel loving toward, we can confess our lack of love, resist our human feelings, yield ourselves to Christ and ask that He make us able to love.

Agape love makes it possible to experience unfailing love in marriage. No marriage need ever die for lack of love. If love appears to have cooled, the answer is confession, repentance and a willingness to stand on God's principle. The problem may be rough, but God's provision is secured for us by Christ.

Jesus commanded us to love—even our enemies. He would not have done so if the provision was not already available.

Look again at Peter's nine principles. See how they are linked together progressively. They can only be developed one by one, little by little. One friend typed these on a card, linking each principle to the next one with an arrow, and placed the list next to the bathroom mirror. Each morning provided an opportunity for check-up. How would you measure up against this reminder?

Peter concludes his thoughts with the following

encouragements and promises:

> For if these qualities are yours and are increasing, they render you neither useless nor unfruitful in the true knowledge of our Lord Jesus Christ. For he who lacks these qualities is blind or short-sighted, having forgotten his purification from his former sins. Therefore, brethren, be all the more diligent to make certain about His calling and choosing you; for as long as you practice these things, you will never stumble; for in this way the entrance into the eternal kingdom of our Lord and Savior Jesus Christ will be abundantly supplied to you (2 Pet. 1:8-11).

Did you notice the encouragements? We can be fruitful and useful to our Lord. We can live strong, good lives. If we don't go after these qualities which Christ has provided for us, we're short-sighted, wandering in the wilderness, suffering and stumbling. God's intention is to bring us into the promised land. Anyone who doesn't eagerly accept that opportunity is very foolish, indeed, says Peter.

But when you have allowed Christ to develop these nine principles in your life, you will never, *ever* fall. There will be nothing in your heart that will cause you to stumble when temptation comes knocking at your door.

The Bible tells us that instant possession of the promised land, or instant spiritual maturity, is impossible. This isn't because God isn't capable of giving it to us all at once, but because if He did, we would be destroyed. Listen to Moses as he explains God's plan to the Israelites:

> And the Lord your God will clear away these

nations before you little by little; you will not be able to put an end to them quickly, lest the wild beasts grow too numerous for you (Deut. 7:22).

Our promised land can become ours a little at a time, because we too must have time to grow in ability to possess it.

chapter eleven

What Is the Promised Land?

W hat shall I render to the Lord for all His benefits toward me? I shall lift up the cup of salvation, and call upon the name of the Lord'' (Ps. 116:12,13). The Lord gave me this psalm as a promise. I was overwhelmed with His mercy and His goodness. I was feeling as if He had indeed daily loaded me with benefits, and I was searching to know how I could best return His love, how I could express to Him my overflowing sense of gratitude. Suddenly, impressed on my mind were these two verses and this clear statement: "He loves Me best who seeks to enter and enjoy all that I suffered and died for."

Which one of us, upon discovering God's grace, the extent of His love and the all-encompassing nature of His redemption, hasn't wanted to give the Lord something in return? How can we be satisfied to enjoy or teach a minimized salvation when Christ suffered for a maximized redemption that includes all of life? Something planted deeply within me refused to dishonor the magnitude of the Master's plan by reducing it to less than full biblical proportion.

What then can I do? Drink deeply of the cup of salvation. That is, I can explore all that Christ biblically and clearly provided, then set myself by the four Ps to obtain and attain all that I can in my lifetime: my promised land.

Anyone who embarks on a deeper-than-surface reading of the Bible will soon discover the promised land in chapter 8 of the book of Romans. We have already discussed some of the features of our promised land. It is not primarily a geographical location as in Exodus but a physical and spiritual reality. It is a place of rest where we have ceased from our own labors and are able to enjoy the provisions God has made for us. It is a land where we will dwell in cities we didn't build, enjoy fruit from orchards we didn't plant, drink water from wells we didn't dig. The physical provisions of the promised land include material possessions and health—all that we need for meeting the demands of the day. But these come about as a direct result of the spiritual provision God has made possible. When we possess the spiritual reality of the promised land, the milk and honey (an abundance of all we need) will flow.

The spiritual reality of our promised land is described in Romans 8. Here is assurance that we, as Christians, may live a life without guilt and condemnation, a life as joint heirs with Christ. All things may work out for our best. God will give us freely of all things. We can be more than conquerors through Him. Nothing can ever separate us from God's love in Christ. The entire chapter is a tremendous declaration of the victorious Christian life God has made available to us.

A friend once told me, ''Most people know about Romans 8, but I live there.'' This is God's desire for us. He wants every one of the provisions of that chapter to function in our lives daily. We may learn to recite it from memory, but that will not insure our inhabiting the land of plenty and overflowing. How do we get there?

We go back again to our Law of the Four Ps. We have learned to look for a promise, principle and problem prior to the provision. In the book of Romans, this pattern is demonstrated. Look at the chart below. Seen in this perspective, four chapters fall into line with amazing clarity. They should be studied in sequence. Here we will focus merely on the key verses.

PROMISE	PRINCIPLE	PROBLEM	PROVISION
Chapter 5	Chapter 6	Chapter 7	Chapter 8

The Promise

For if, because of one man's trespass (lapse, offense) death reigned through that one, much more surely will those who receive [God's] overflowing grace (unmerited favor) and the free gift of righteousness (putting them into right standing with Himself) reign as kings in life through the One, Jesus Christ, the Messiah, the Anointed One (Rom. 5:17, Amplified).

Here is our promise: We will reign as kings in this life. The promise is for right now—not for some future date when Christ returns. We are to reign over the circumstances in which we find ourselves—at home, work, school, everywhere. We are to reign amidst conflict, confusion and problems.

The Principle

How the promise is to become reality is already indicated: We are to "reign" through the One, Jesus Christ. Chapter 6 spells out in detail both why and how this is possible. First the why:

> For if we have become one with Him by sharing a death like His, we shall also be [one with Him in sharing] His resurrection [by a new life lived for God]. We know that our old (unrenewed) self was nailed to the cross with Him in order that [our] body, [which is the instrument] of sin, might be made ineffective *and* inactive for evil, that we might no longer be the slaves of sin (vv. 5,6, Amplified).

Our lives as reigning kings have been made possible by what Christ has already done for us. His substitutionary death for us is a past reality, an established fact. By accepting what He has done for us personally, we are indeed dead in the sense that our natural, sin-loving self no longer rules over us. We no longer need to be slaves of sin; that is, we have been given the ability to choose. Now the option is ours, and the principle tells us how we can use it:

> So look upon your old sin nature as dead and unresponsive to sin, and instead be alive to God, alert to him, through Jesus Christ our Lord. Do not let sin control your puny body any longer; do not give in to its sinful desires. Do not let any part of your bodies become tools of wickedness, to be used for sinning; but give yourself completely to God—every part of you—for you are back from

death and you want to be tools in the hand of God, to be used for his good purpose (vv. 11-13, TLB).

Notice the action words: *look* upon, *be* alive, do not *let*, do not *give* in, *give* yourself completely, *to be used* by God. We are told to do basically two things. *Refuse* to respond in the old way to sinful desires; and *give* ourselves totally to God.

The Problem

The problem is put between the principle and the provision in order to reveal any tendency in us to do our own thing instead of abiding by God's instructions. The problem Paul describes is a common one for all of us. It is what happens once we've become aware of God's will and find ourselves incapable of doing it.

So I find it to be a law [of my being] that when I want to do what is right *and* good, evil is ever present with me *and* I am subject to its insistent demands. For I endorse *and* delight in the Law of God in my inmost self—with my new nature. [Ps. 1:2.] But I discern in my bodily members—in the sensitive appetites and wills of the flesh—a different law (rule of action) at war against the law of my mind (my reason) and making me a prisoner to the law of sin that dwells in my bodily organs—in the sensitive appetites and wills of the flesh. O unhappy *and* pitiable *and* wretched man that I am! Who will release *and* deliver me from [the shackles of] this body of death?'' (Rom. 7:21-24, Amplified).

To reveal any hidden "Pharisees" or rule-keepers, in our hearts, God places us in situations where our own efforts at being good, fair or loving will hopelessly fail. I have always desired to be a good father and a loving husband, but didn't know how. When I have wanted to be patient, pure, honest, I found it impossible in my own strength. There have also been times when I wanted my family and neighbors to see a Christlike nature in me, and I have struggled to overcome the personal failures I know are unfit for someone who is supposed to "reign in this life."

I have seen other Christians in this same battle. I know there are millions who struggle with their hidden envy, pride, resentment, covetousness or other powerful tendencies that keep them bound and suffering in the wilderness of their problems.

The Provision

But when our knowledge and practice of the principle have become tested and refined through the problem, we are able to enter the promised land—in this case, chapter 8 of Romans.

When the second-generation Israelites entered Canaan, they found that each piece of the land had to be possessed separately. In other words, the principles and the problem had to come before each individual section of land could become theirs. In our individual Christian experience, we have to possess "the land" in the same manner.

In the first four verses of chapter 8, we have three "pieces" of our promised inheritance:

Therefore [there is] now no condemnation—no adjudging guilty of wrong—for those who are in Christ Jesus, *who live not after the dictates of the flesh but after the dictates of the Spirit.* For the law of the Spirit of life [which is] in Christ Jesus [the law of our new being], has freed me from the law of sin and of death. For God has done what the Law could not do, [its power] being weakened by the flesh [that is, the entire nature of man without the Holy Spirit]. Sending His own Son in the guise of sinful flesh and as an offering for sin, [God] condemned sin in the flesh—subdued, overcame, deprived it of its power [over all who accept that sacrifice]. So that the righteous *and* just requirement of the Law might be fully met in us, who live *and* move not in the ways of the flesh but in the ways of the Spirit—our lives governed not by the standards *and* according to the dictates of the flesh, but controlled by the (Holy) Spirit (Amplified).

In short, our inheritance means:

1. *We can live without condemnation.*

2. *We can be free from the vicious circle of sin and death.*

3. *We can obey God's laws!*

These can become spiritual realities as we apply the principle, resist our old nature, submit to God and let Christ live in us and for us.

The problem will confront us with the temptation to do otherwise. The religious question will be aimed at us: "What do you mean, no condemnation? You're guilty and you know it. You're not good enough, you're not free from sin, and you certainly aren't obeying God's laws! You better try a little harder to be good." If we crumple up and submit to the guilt—seek to pray more—study more—strive to please—we are forced to take another lap around the mountain.

Instead of giving in to our guilt feelings, we may practice God's principle and respond, "Sure I am guilty. But Christ is without guilt, and it is His life in me that gives me right standing with God. I want to do God's will. I won't give in to my old doubts and guilt feelings.

I trust Jesus to change me. I am *not* under condemnation. I am free from the vicious circle of sin and death, and I am obeying God's law in Christ—and this regardless of how often I slip or how guilty I feel." With this response, we will soon come to experience the reality of freedom from guilt and condemnation.

There are twenty other "pieces" of land included in our inheritance as presented in Romans 8. We shall look briefly at each of these, thus getting some idea of the wonderful provisions that are ours for the taking.

4. *We can be God-pleasers.*

For those who are according to the flesh *and* controlled by its unholy desires, set their minds on *and* pursue those things which gratify the flesh. But those who are according to the Spirit *and* [controlled by the desires] of the Spirit, set their minds on *and* seek those things which gratify the (Holy) Spirit (v.5, Amplified).

Ever since becoming a Christian, I have *wanted* to please God and I have discovered (the hard way, resulting in many laps around the mountain) that I cannot possibly please God no matter how hard I try. Mercifully, God has provided a way. If we follow His instructions, we'll find ourselves doing things that please Him.

5. *We can have life and soul-peace.*

Now the mind of the flesh [which is sense and reason without the Holy Spirit,] is death—death that comprises all the miseries arising from sin, both here and hereafter. But the mind of the (Holy) Spirit is life and soul-peace [both now and forever] (v.6, Amplified).

How we all long for peace! Soul-peace is a peace that comes through our spirit to saturate our whole being,

personality, mind and emotions. It means peace instead
of frustration, tension, worry or restlessness. It means
quietness in the midst of our turbulent world. It is meant
to be ours in Christ.

6. *The indwelling Holy Spirit can control us.*
You are controlled by your new nature if you have
the Spirit of God living in you. (And remember
that if anyone doesn't have the Spirit of Christ living in him, he is not a Christian at all) (v.9, TLB).

We know from experience that it is possible to be a
Christian, indwelt by the Holy Spirit, and yet not let
the Holy Spirit control our lives. Control by the Holy
Spirit is not an automatic feature of the Christian life.
It can only come when we give up self-will, resist the
control of our sinful nature and turn ourselves over to
Christ. This is not done once and for all by a single decision. Rather it must be repeated daily, often in the heat
of a problem.

7. *The Spirit can quicken our mortal bodies.*
And if the Spirit of Him Who raised up Jesus from
the dead dwells in you, [then] He Who raised up
Christ *Jesus* from the dead will also restore to life
your mortal (short-lived, perishable) bodies
through His Spirit Who dwells in you (v. 11,
Amplified).

This is not only a promise of life after death, but rather
a promise of physical ''quickening'' or divine provision for our physical sickness and weakness. He is saying that our puny mortal bodies can be quickened, given
a new life, a new surge of health and energy right now.

8. *We can put to death the evil deeds of our body.*
...if through the power of the (Holy) Spirit you put
to death—make extinct, deaden—the [evil] deeds

prompted by the body, you shall (really and genuinely) live forever (v. 13, Amplified).

Do you see how it is done? The principle is at work when we habitually put to death (resist and deny) the old habits and turn ourselves over to Christ.

9. *We can be led by the Spirit of God.*

For all who are led by the Spirit of God are sons of God (v. 14, Amplified).

10. *We can know the Spirit of adoption.*

For [the Spirit which] you have now received [is] not a spirit of slavery to put you once more in bondage to fear, but you have received the Spirit of adoption—the Spirit producing sonship—in [the bliss of] which we cry, Abba! [That is,] Father! (v. 15, Amplified).

11. *The Spirit can tell us that we are His child.*

For his Holy Spirit speaks to us deep in our hearts and tells us that we really are God's children (v. 16, TLB).

This assurance is provided for us, but you can imagine the problem and the religious question putting it to the test.

12. *We can be joint heirs with Christ.*

And since we are his children, we shall share his treasures—for all God gives to His Son Jesus is now ours too... (v. 17, TLB).

13. *Glorious freedom from sin.*

For on that day thorns and thistles, sin, death and decay—the things that overcame the world against its will at God's command—will all disappear, and the world around us will share in the glorious freedom from sin which God's children enjoy (vv. 20,21, TLB).

Paul is talking about the complete freedom from sin we will enjoy in the future, after the resurrection. But he also speaks of a substantial freedom from sin which God's children can enjoy even today.

14. *The redemption of our bodies.*

And even we Christians, although we have the Holy Spirit within us as a foretaste of future glory, also groan to be released from pain and suffering. We, too, wait anxiously for that day when God will give us full rights as his children, including the new bodies he has promised us—bodies that will never be sick again and will never die (v. 23, TLB).

Provisions 13 and 14 are the only ones we can't experience fully until the day when Christ comes again. Nevertheless, there is even now some measure of fulfillment here. Even our present-day, dying bodies can experience greater life than most of us know.

15. *The Spirit can help with our daily problems and prayers.*

And in the same way—by our faith—the Holy Spirit helps us with our daily problems and in our praying. For we don't even know what we should pray for, nor how to pray as we should; but the Holy Spirit prays for us with such feeling that it cannot be expressed in words (v. 26, TLB).

16. *We can know that everything happens for our good.*

And we know that all that happens to us is working for our good if we love God and are fitting into his plans (v. 28, TLB).

Many Christians quote this verse but are unable to see their problems as part of God's plan for their good. God's plan is to bring us from the promise into the provision. The problem doesn't pop up to thwart God's intentions, but is an inevitable part of His plan. All that happens to us is meant to work for our good, including the things that we have habitually called bad. This springs from our old nature, our reason and our understanding without the Holy Spirit's enlightening. We must deliberately resist these old thought patterns, confess them as sin, ask God to take them away and replace them with the ability to look at all things as part of His good plan. This ability is ours in Christ.

17. *We can become conformed to Christ's image.*
For from the very beginning God decided that those who came to him—and all along He knew who would—should become like his Son, so that his Son would be the First, with many brothers (v. 29, TLB).

You and I cannot live Christlike lives by trying to be like Him. We can only be like Him to the degree that He lives His life in us.

18. *We can know that God is always on our side.*
What can we say to such wonderful things as these? If God is on our side, who can ever be against us? (v. 31, TLB).

Have you ever felt that you were alone against the whole world? Moses faced the whole nation of Israel who wanted to stone him and return to Egypt. But God was with Moses, and God always constitutes the majority of One. He has made the provision to be always on our side, but in the middle of the problem it may not seem that way!

19. *God will freely give us all things.*
Since he did not spare even his own Son for us but gave him up for us all, won't he also surely give

us everything else? (v. 32, TLB).

20. *Christ will plead our cause.*

Who then will condemn us? Will Christ? *No!* For he is the one who died for us and came back to life again for us and is sitting at the place of highest honor next to God, pleading for us there in heaven (v. 34, TLB).

Christ is pleading our cause, but we cannot receive the full benefits of this provision until we yield ourselves to Him. If we remain stubborn in our self-sufficiency, we cannot receive what Christ has won for us.

21. *Nothing can keep Christ's love from us.*

Who then can ever keep Christ's love from us? When we have trouble or calamity, when we are hunted down or destroyed, is it because he doesn't love us anymore? And if we are hungry, or penniless, or in danger, or threatened with death, has God deserted us? No, for the Scriptures tell us that for his sake we must be ready to face death at every moment of the day—we are like sheep awaiting slaughter (vv. 35,36, TLB).

This list of circumstances sounds like a very inclusive description to any wilderness area we might encounter. The religious question in the midst of temptation will always suggest that this is proof that God has left us or doesn't love us. On the contrary, it is only *through* very difficult circumstances that we can learn to rely on God's constant presence and never-ending love.

22. *We can be more than conquerors.*

Yet amid all these things we are more than conquerors *and* gain a surpassing victory through Him Who loved us (v. 37, Amplified).

The victory is always ours through Christ, because

it simply cannot be won any other way.

23. *Nothing can separate us from God's love.*
For I am convinced that nothing can ever separate us from his love. Death can't and life can't. The angels won't and all the powers of hell itself cannot keep God's love away. Our fears for today, our worries about tomorrow, or where we are—high above the sky, or in the deepest ocean—nothing will ever be able to separate us from the love of God demonstrated by our Lord Jesus Christ when he died for us (vv. 38,39, TLB).

Here is our promised land, where we are meant to live—not just in one area of it, and not for just a visit when we feel spiritual, but always. Many Christians share Paul's problem in chapter 7. They know what God wants them to do, but they flounder in the problem, unable to obey. But remember, our goal is to become permanent residents in the promised land!

chapter twelve

Personal Conduct in Temptation

The whole church of Jesus Christ needs to be taught that there are two conquests: *the conquest of sin*, of greed and pollution, and *the conquest of Satan*. Neither can be neglected and both are necessary to enjoy the full provision of the promised land. There are then *two* factors with which we must contend in temptation: the atoning work of Jesus Christ and the real, ultimate defeat of the devil.

After we have been reconciled to God, provision must be made whereby we can be nourished, instructed and taught the victorious nature of Christian living. As someone said, "Because we live in this world, Christ has given us an inescapable obligation of participating in society." Jesus prayed, asking His Father: "I do not ask Thee to take them out of the world, but to keep them from the evil one" (John 17:15). As the whole church faces its failure and sin effectively, it will begin to believe that the defeat of satanic power is a genuine possibility in this life. Then, gradually but surely, we will believe that Christ can "crush Satan under our feet," achieving personal victory over sin and defeating satanic deception in our families, schools and nation. We can see him defeated in two realms, not just one. This is not the "millennium on earth," but the fruit of a healthy, active church that knows evil is socially mediated (see 1 Cor. 15:33).

The biblical model says, "I must get on with the Lord, learn to know and use the Scriptures, understand what it means to pray in the Spirit and otherwise increase in spiritual strength as Paul teaches in Ephesians 6:10, 'Be strong in the Lord, and in the power of His might,' if I am to endure trials and temptation." The purpose of this goal is not so that you can be a display-case model of the victorious Christian life, but rather that you can get on with the marching orders of the Master, "Go and make disciples of all nations" (Matt. 28:19). The passage on the armor of God and Christian victory ends on the same note: "Be on the alert...pray on my behalf, that utterance may be given to me in the opening of my mouth, to make known with boldness the mystery of the gospel" (Eph. 6:18,19).

As each of us, individually and then corporately, seeks to enter God's "land of promises," we find ourselves facing formidable adversaries. There is a declared enmity between the seed of woman (Christ) and the seed of the serpent (Satan) which cannot be negotiated. That enmity is the unrelenting desire of the satanic hosts to take advantage of God's people. Because Satan cannot touch Christ, his fury is vented toward the body of Christ. He has no intention of relinquishing his hold over the minds of men and women without a bitter struggle. God has promised to drive out our enemies from before us, little by little. The large war has been won, but our participation and personal conduct do determine the outcome of the immediate battle.

Biblical history abounds with case histories demonstrating that when God's people obeyed and trusted Him completely, He never failed to win the battle for them. Let me hasten to add, victory or not, it was a real battle. It is equally true that when they disobeyed and moved in human presumption they were always defeated. May we learn the lesson as well as the story!

Again, our example is the Israelites. The story of how they came to possess their biblical Promised Land, little by little, demonstrates the same principle over and over again: When they obeyed God and trusted Him completely, He always won the battle for them; when they relied on their own strength, they lost. Joshua and Jehoshaphat were two leaders who led their armies to victory by obeying and trusting God.

The story of the battle of Jericho is told in Joshua 6. God told Joshua to commandeer his forces and march around the fortified city seven times in seven days. On the last day they were to blow their trumpets and the walls would come tumbling down—and they did! Archeologists have dug at the site of old Jericho and found the remains of an old city wall which apparently fell outward as the result of an earthquake or other powerful force. What happened at Jericho is verifiable fact, not an old myth or fairy tale.

Later, Jehoshaphat and his men faced the multitudes of the armies of Moab, Ammon and Mount Seit. But God told them: ''Do not fear or be dismayed because of this great multitude, for the battle is not yours but God's'' (2 Chron. 20:15). We read that God instructed Jehoshaphat to place his band of singers and musicians in full view of the enemy forces, and while they sang praises to Jehovah, He turned the enemy armies against each other until they had completely destroyed each other. The Israelites didn't receive a scratch.

The battle was God's, but the outcome depended on the conduct of the Israelites during the fighting. Had they doubted God's word and involved themselves in the fighting, He could not have kept them from harm. God can only fight our battles if we follow His instructions and trust Him for the outcome.

Our preparation for the battles God has promised to win for us consists of learning to get our own selves out of the way so that we can rely totally on God.

As we look back over the wilderness, over the problems and the temptations, we recognize that it is all part of the preparation for the battles to possess the promised land.

When the young army recruit first comes to boot camp, he's half-scared because he doesn't know what is expected of him. He gets his verbal and written instructions first. Then come the exercises to develop his physical and emotional endurance and his ability to handle weapons. By the time he is through with training, he's eager to see some action and test in practice the principles he has been taught.

The young Christian is a recruit in the army of the Lord. The terminology of warfare is used throughout the Bible to emphasize the very real battle between the forces of good and evil. The Christian life is to be on the front lines, although the battle isn't ours—but God's.

Our preparations for battle start with the written instructions from God's Word. We need to know what is expected of us and how God works. Then the rough part of the training comes when we move into problems and temptations to develop our endurance and test what we have learned.

God continues to offer opportunities for growth. He feeds us and strengthens us daily with His Word. Whenever we are presented with fresh teaching and messages, we should be on the alert to drink them in and make them a part of our equipment, for we may be certain that we are going to need it as we move forward to battle. When we understand the principle and know what is expected of us, we can move with eager anticipation into the subsequent phases of our training.

James Describes God's Ways

James experienced the joy of being prepared for battle in his day. Let's take a close look at what he says (James 1:2-8), as his insights will help us be victorious in battle. To claim that victory, we do not need a stronger will, but deeper insight into God's ways.

Verse 2: "Consider it all joy, my brethren, when you encounter various trials." Why should we consider it joy (in Greek it is a command, not a suggestion)? When, by no fault of our own, we are brought into a test/temptation, we can, we *must*, rejoice, for we have been given an opportunity to demonstrate our faithfulness to the Lord (see John 14:21). Nothing, may I suggest, gives greater joy than to be victorious in spiritual battle!

Verses 3-4: "Knowing that the testing of your faith produces endurance. And let endurance have its perfect result, that you may be perfect and complete, lacking in nothing." This is another reminder of the purpose of temptation. First, tested faith is so much better than untested faith, for we never know what or how it works until the test-flight. Second, the test produces an endurance, or the ability to stand after everyone else has collapsed. As St. Gregory so wisely said, we "are sometimes the more firmly established by being shaken." Third, endurance, as it grows and matures, produces Christian character (full grown, complete, lacking nothing). Christian character is what enables you to discipline the senses and walk by principle.

All of life is designed by God for a "shake down cruise." The most advanced and sleekest airplane must face the ultimate question, "Will it fly? What can it do? Can we depend on it?" Both the natural and the spiritual require periodic tests. One student who had been in school for years was asked what his major was. His response, "Taking tests!" Until we know the difference between what we think we have, what we think we know, and what we actually know, we are of little use to God and His kingdom. Another way of saying this is "Don't trust anyone in the realm of the Holy Spirit who doesn't walk with a limp."

Verses 5-6: "But if any of you lacks wisdom, let him ask of God, who gives to all men generously and without reproach, and it will be given to him. But let him ask in faith without any doubting, for the one who doubts is like the surf of the sea driven and tossed by the wind." This marvelous promise is sometimes misunderstood. It might read, "If you lack wisdom, regarding conduct in the trial, ask." God has a real investment in your success, and He will give generously. To ask in faith (regarding the trial) means you have ceased whining, murmuring and acting in a petulant and childish manner.

Not being sure that you want to be victorious or feeling sure that you can't win is being double-minded and is the way to sure defeat.

Verse 7: "For let not that man expect that he will receive anything from the Lord." God refuses to respond to the student in the school of temptation who refuses to learn the lessons. We must decide whether our journeys will be cyclical or linear, whether we'll take another trip around the mountain or go into the promised land.

Verse 8: "Being a double-minded man, unstable in all his ways." The fact is, the person who will not take God's clear instructions regarding temptation, will, in fact, refuse His instruction in other areas of life, especially if they do not suit his or her fancy. Thus, we are back to the nature of law-less-ness: asserting my own will as the preferred rule of action over and against the known will of God. Such people do not have Christian character. They will demonstrate instability in every area of their spiritual lives, and, most probably, in their natural existence as well. Such people become cyclical and not linear. These people are also given to what I call the "Butterfly Syndrome," for they move from relationship to relationship, job to job, church to church, even geographically from location to location. They go through the four-month "honeymoon period" and then hit reality. Rather than endure, they switch. Thus, in biblical understanding, they "receive nothing from the Lord."

Paul's Advice for Battle Preparation

We are ready for battle when we have gone through problems and temptations that have stripped us of our self-dependency and taught us to depend solely on God for strength.

Another of the leaders of the early church, Paul, left us some challenging words on battle preparation.

> Finally, be strong in the Lord, and in the strength of His might. Put on the full armor of God, that you may be able to stand firm against the schemes of the devil. For our struggle is not against flesh and blood, but against the rulers, against the powers, against the world forces of this darkness, against the spiritual forces of wickedness in the heavenly places (Eph. 6:10-12).

A few years ago, most Christians in our Western "civilized" world thought Paul expressed the unenlightened and superstitious beliefs of his age when he described our enemies as "mighty satanic beings, great evil princes of darkness and wicked spirits." Today we are seeing increasing evidence of how real the powers of darkness are and what formidable enemies they can be. Those who have fought the desperate battles against drug addiction, alcoholism or homosexuality, to mention only three areas where the powers of darkness are at work, have discovered that it is impossible to be victorious in their own strength. If these battles are to be won at all, they must be won by God.

The forces of darkness are actively at work in rebellion, crime, marriage breakups, sickness and many other ills from which we suffer. But the outcome hangs in the delicate balance between the individual, God and the forces of evil. Jesus Christ has already won the battle for us. Satan is defeated. But in each situation, the outcome depends on personal response. If one chooses to resist evil and yield totally to God, He will fight and win the battles for us.

Paul has some further advice for us with some specifics for getting ready to meet the enemy.

Therefore, take up the full armor of God, that you may be able to resist in the evil day, and having done everything, to stand firm. Stand firm therefore, having girded your loins with truth, and having put on the breastplate of righteousness, and having shod your feet with the preparation of the gospel of peace, in addition to all, taking up the shield of faith with which you will be able to extinguish all the flaming missiles of the evil one (Eph. 6:13-16).

A Lesson From Joshua

Everything we need to stand in the battle is provided for us. We don't have to be clever or strong or super-spiritual. We only need to rely on Jesus Christ. Be happy when you find yourself moving into a battle, because the outcome will reveal one of two things: If you stand, it shows that you have absorbed what you need of the Christ-life to receive your provision of victory; if you fall, you can be happy, as well—because the battle has revealed what is really in your heart and what you need for facing the next battle! It is a great deal better to discover any weaknesses so that they may be adjusted, rather than to have it revealed in eternity! If there is anger, resentment or pride in your heart, and this is keeping you from claiming your rightful possession of the promised land—wouldn't you rather find out about it now?

God allowed Joshua to lose a battle in order to show him that there was a hidden sin in the camp. Once that sin was exposed and removed, God led Joshua into battle with the same enemy and gave him victory. The story is recorded in Joshua 7 and 8.

After the battle at Jericho, God gave the Israelites specific instructions not to keep any battle loot for themselves. One of Joshua's men, Achan, couldn't resist a beautiful robe, stole it and hid it in the ground under his tent.

Later Joshua sent some of his men to spy on the city of Ai. They returned with the report that it was a small city and wouldn't take more than two or three thousand of them to destroy it.

The Israelites, confident after their easy victory at Jericho, marched up against Ai and were soundly defeated.

Joshua had gone into battle unaware of the hidden sin in his camp. But he had also made a mistake himself. He had neglected to consult God before going up against this new enemy. If we turn to God *before* a battle and pray, "Lord, let there not be any hidden sin in me that will cause You to have to lead me into temptation— reveal that hidden sin now," then God is able to show us any trouble point without putting us through a losing battle.

Realizing immediately that God had permitted the defeat in order to show him something, Joshua turned in repentance and God told him about Achan's sin. The culprit was brought into the open and he and his entire family destroyed.

> Don't be afraid or discouraged; take the entire army and go to Ai, for it is now yours to conquer. I have given the king of Ai and all of his people to you. You shall do to them as you did to Jericho and her king; but this time you may keep the loot and the cattle for yourselves (Josh. 8:1,2, TLB).

Why had God made the ruling against taking loot at Jericho? Because He knew the weakness, spirit of disobedience and greed in Achan. He permitted the temptation to bring the weakness out into the open. Once the weakness was exposed and repented of, God told Joshua not to be discouraged or afraid.

When we suffer defeat in battle, we should realize that God permits it to show us a weakness which He wants to replace with His strength. We should not be discouraged or afraid, for God never reveals our weakness in order to condemn us. He simply gives us opportunity to rid ourselves of our old nature so that we may replace it with the divine nature He has promised us.

Therefore, we can rejoice in our defeats and failures, knowing that the ultimate end God desires for us is good. I have often learned as much (if not more) from a failure as from a success.

Victory in Defeat?

Defeats serve as a reminder (as it did in the case of Joshua and his men) that all is not well in our camp. We may roll along fairly smoothly, oblivious to our own tendencies to self-willed rebellion, until we stumble and fall in a battle. We should thank God right then and there for reminding us that we need Him. A defeat or failure is designed to bring us back to God. If we are not certain what caused the trouble, we must say as David did:

Search me, O God, and know my heart; try me and know my anxious thoughts; and see if there be any hurtful way in me, and lead me in the everlasting way (Ps. 139:23,24).

First, we must return to God; second, we must confess that we are at fault. Even when we do not know our specific mistake, we must, like Joshua, repent. For we know that if we had followed given instructions and relied totally on the life and strength of Christ, victory would have been assured. Christ cannot fail. When we fail, it is because of our wrongdoing at some point.

Repentance leads to renewal. Hear David as he prayed following his discovery of wrongdoing.

> I admit my shameful deed—it haunts me day and night....You saw it all, and your sentence against me is just....Sprinkle me with the cleansing blood and I shall be clean again. Wash me and I shall be whiter than snow. And after you have punished me [after my defeat], give me back my joy again....Create in me a new, clean heart, O God, filled with clean thoughts and right desires (Ps. 51:3-10, TLB).

A clean heart and a new nature are part of the promised land. Little by little God exposes and renews our hearts. We couldn't take a complete overhaul at once. One by one, the compartments where there is selfishness—fear, greed, lust, idolatry, jealousy and other trouble spots—will be brought out into the open, cleansed and renewed. This gives place to the new nature—love, joy, peace, kindness, patience, goodness, faithfulness, gentleness and self-control!

Look at your failures as opportunities for growth, bringing you closer to God. Pick yourself up and say, "Sorry I missed it again, Lord. Show me. Teach me. Change me." As we learn to trust ourselves less and Christ more, and as we learn to come to Him before the battle starts, we can be assured of increasing victories.

Remember, God will give us wisdom if we ask for

it. He wants us to go into battle fully prepared as to how to conduct ourselves. When we have learned how to turn the promise of wisdom into provision, we can come to God and say, "Lord, I see I am getting into a battle. I don't want to squirm out of it. I want to go through it in Your strength and I want You to tell me how to conduct myself while I am in the problem." God will give us wisdom when we ask for it. That is a promise.

But we must apply the principle of faith through the problem. We must believe that God can and will supply the wisdom. The problem will present us with the temptation to doubt and waver, and the outcome will be decided by us. We must resist the doubting and wavering and yield ourselves to Him who can supply the faith to take us through to provision and victory.

The Victory Is Ours

After victory in the battle we will reign as kings in life. James 1:12 says, "Blessed is a man who perseveres under trial; for once he has been approved, he will receive the crown of life, which the Lord has promised to those who love Him." Blessed, or to be envied, is the person who has learned the spiritual skill of endurance under trial or temptation.

How do we gain God's approval? By passing the test, by winning the battle. There is an obscure reference to a man in Romans 16:10 whom I hope to meet in eternity one day. It says simply, "Greet Appeles, the approved in Christ"! Paul says to Timothy, "Study to shew thyself approved" (2 Tim. 2:15, KJV), or applauded after testing. The crown of life relates back to Romans 5:17 when Paul promised us that we can "reign in life"—and that means more than mere existence in this life or the promise of a golden life in heaven!

The provision is ours—the promised land with cities we didn't build, wells we didn't dig and orchards we didn't plant. There we are to experience financial security, marital joy, rest in God's care. This is the place of rest where we can do all things through Christ who strengthens us. There will be enemies and problems, but we are reigning over them in the peace and strength Christ affords.

Years ago, a phone call came to my office. Our four-year-old son had been taken to the emergency room at the hospital. Rushing there, I found my wife, Judy, at his bedside. He had been struck by a car while playing outside our home and had received cuts, bruises and a fractured femur at the base of the pelvis.

As we stood by his bedside, the temptation came to feel that we were being punished by God. Instead, Judy and I were both swept with joy and an awareness of God's tremendous love for us and our son.

Standing in the emergency room with hands raised before the Lord in gratitude, we came to understand what it means to "consider it wholly joyful...whenever you are enveloped in or encounter trials of any sort, or fall into various temptations" (James 1:2, Amplified). The wonderful provision from Romans 8 was ours.

Who can then keep Christ's love from us when we have trouble or calamity? When our little boy is hit by a car and seriously injured?

No, nothing will ever be able to separate us from the love of God demonstrated by our Lord Jesus Christ when He died for us. This is provision—and it is ours to claim!

As Christians and spiritual Israelites, we are not meant

to be permanent wilderness-wanderers. Maturity demands the recognition and use of the four Ps in the face of temptation!

APPENDIX
WILDERNESS IN THE BIBLE
The Four Ps Illustrated

	Promise	Principle	Problem	Provision
1 Adam and Eve Genesis 2,3	Fellowship with God, the Garden of Eden	Obedience to God's command	Satanic temptation	Failed
2 Abraham Genesis 12-22	Father of nations	Faith and obedience	Years of waiting, laps in problem	"Father of the Faith"
3 Isaac Genesis 25	Promised a son	Willingness and obedience	Twenty years childless	Birth of Jacob and Esau
4 Jacob Genesis 29	Marriage to Rachel	Obedience to Laban	Deception and injustice	Rachel as bride
5 Joseph Genesis 37-45	Dream of greatness	Faith and obedience	Sold into slavery, jail and suffering	Rescued his people from famine
6 Moses Exodus 2-14	To deliver his people	Faith and obedience	Kills Egyptian, years in exile	Delivers his people from Egypt
7 Israel Exodus, Leviticus, Numbers, Deuteronomy	The Promised Land	Willingness and obedience	Forty years in wilderness	First generation failed
8 Job Job	Perfection of faith	Trust and obedience	Spiritual and physical testing	Faith, abundant restoration
9 David 1 Samuel 16-31	To be king	Obedience to will of God	Persecution by Saul in wilderness	Anointed king
10 Every Man Psalm 23	Cup running over, anointing	Faith in Good Shepherd	Valley of death	Eternal blessings

11 Maiden Song of Solomon	Marriage to the king	Willingness to follow king	Wilderness experiences	Belonging to the beloved
12 Messiah Isaiah 52 and 53	Shall be exalted	Obedience to will of God	Despised, rejected, grief and sorrow	Receive a portion with the great
13 Christ Luke 4	Savior	Obedience to God's Word	Temptation in wilderness	Messianic fullness
14 Mary Luke 1	Mother of our Lord	Faith and obedience	Humiliation, misunderstanding	Honor and recognition
15 Peter Luke 22	Keys to kingdom	Submission and faith	Denial of his Lord	Restored and established
16 Disciples Luke 24	Authority and witness	Stability in faith	Crucifixion of Christ	Meeting the resurrected Christ
17 N.T. church Acts 20	Preach pure gospel of repentance and faith in Christ	Hold fast to pure doctrine	Division, grievous wolves	Inheritance of those who are set apart (see v. 32)
18 Paul Philippians 1	Apostle of Jesus Christ	Faith, obedience and humility	Persecution, beatings, prison, suffering	Prize of his high calling of God in Christ (see Phil. 3:14)
19 Timothy 1 and 2 Timothy	Usefulness in God's work	Faith, diligence, obedience	Spiritual warfare, false teachers	Strength and boldness, full provision
20 Christian life Galatians 2:20	Freedom from bondage	Christ in us	Dying to self	Resurrection life
21 Believers Romans 5-8	Reign in life (Rom. 5)	Dead to self, risen with Christ (Rom. 6)	Conflict between old and new nature (Rom. 7)	The promised land (Rom. 8)

OTHER PUBLICATIONS OF INTEREST FROM CREATION HOUSE

Could You Not Tarry One Hour?
by Larry Lea

To many Christians prayer is a drudgery. Larry Lea has discovered that prayer can be a pleasure and we can learn how to enjoy it. The more we learn to "tarry one hour," the more we will grow in likeness to Christ and the more we will be able to bring His timeless message to a world in pain. $12.95

ISBN 0-88419-198-2   Hardback

Riding the Wind
Your Life in the Holy Spirit
by Everett (Terry) L. Fullam

Raise your sails and let the gentle breezes of the Holy Spirit move in your life. Learn more about Him and His availability to you in this personal and biblical book by one of America's finest teachers. $7.95

ISBN 0-88419-196-6   Trade Paper

Available at your Christian bookstore or from:

190 N. Westmonte Drive
Altamonte Springs, FL 32714
(305) 869-5005